D1049034

The Post-evangelical Debate

The Post-evangelical Debate

Graham Cray, Maggi Dawn, Nick Mercer,
Michael Saward, Pete Ward and Nigel Wright

TRIANGLE

First published in Great Britain 1997
Triangle
Society for Promoting Christian Knowledge
Holy Trinity Church
Marylebone Road
London NW1 4DU

British Library Cataloguing-in-Publication Data
A catalogue record of this book is available
from the British Library

ISBN 0–281–05108–9

Typeset by Pioneer Associates, Perthshire
Printed in Great Britain by
Caledonian International, Glasgow

Contents

Publisher's note   vii

List of contributors   ix

1. The post-evangelical debate   1
   Graham Cray

2. The tribes of evangelicalism   19
   Pete Ward

3. 'You have to change to stay the same'   35
   Maggi Dawn

4. Living intimately with strangers –   57
   a post-evangelical pilgrimage?
   Nick Mercer

5. At root, it's a matter of the theology   75
   Michael Saward

6. Re-imagining evangelicalism   96
   Nigel Wright

   Notes   113

Publisher's note

The Post-Evangelical (Triangle 1995) by Dave Tomlinson
sparked a vigorous debate about the character and direction of British evangelicalism which has continued more
or less non-stop ever since. Here is the next major step in
that debate, as six leading British Christians set out their
response to some of the issues raised by Dave's book.
Some speaking personally, some dealing with wider ideas,
they each present questions and challenges which in turn
demand a response.

List of contributors

Graham Cray is Principal of Ridley Hall Theological College, Cambridge.

Maggi Dawn is an ordinand in the Church of England. She is currently engaged in post-graduate research in theology at Cambridge University.

Nick Mercer, formerly a Baptist minister and Assistant Principal of the London Bible College, is now an Anglican priest.

Michael Saward, Canon and Treasurer of St Paul's Cathedral, is a lifelong evangelical, and an author, broadcaster, journalist and hymnwriter.

Pete Ward is Archbishop of Canterbury's Adviser for Youth Ministry, Visiting Research Fellow at King's College London and Tutor at Oxford Youth Works. He is also the author of *Growing up Evangelical* (SPCK 1996).

Nigel Wright is senior pastor of Altrincham Baptist Church and previously lectured in Christian Doctrine at Spurgeon's College, London.

1 The post-evangelical debate

GRAHAM CRAY

I am grateful to Dave Tomlinson for the courage and clarity shown in writing *The Post-Evangelical*. He has identified the crucial significance of the shift within Western society from 'modern' to 'postmodern' culture and raised a series of key issues which need to be debated by all those who identify themselves in relation to the evangelical tradition.

Any fundamental shift in the cultural context of the Church's mission requires the whole Church to undergo a re-evaluation of most aspects of its life and ministry, even if the result of the questioning were to be 'no change'. *The Post-Evangelical* focuses its readers very clearly upon that task as it faces British evangelicals today. However, it is because my chief concern is for the future of the Church's mission that I have many hesitations about this book's proposals. I acknowledge that the book has acted as a focal point for a significant number of Christians who have identified with its analysis. Dave Tomlinson has allowed them to give themselves a name and to find one another. He has made (some at least) evangelical leaders recognize that their movement has far too many people leaving by the back door at a time when their attention is on the considerable numbers joining through the front door. His book has pastoral and theological importance. But I do not believe his analysis will substantially further the mission of the church.

A *hinge generation?*

I believe the book identifies the particular problems of one
element of a 'hinge' generation; a generation of evangelicals
during a time of culture shift; a generation which was
raised or converted into an evangelical tradition which
was still (quite properly) engaging with modernity, just as
the transition to postmodernity was speeding up and
increasing in visibility. Is it possible that post-evangelicals
are the Generation X or 'baby busters' of the evangelical
world? More importantly, do post-evangelicals hold the
key to Christian mission within postmodernity? Personally
I doubt it.

I totally agree with the starting-point of Dave
Tomlinson's assessment. Western culture is undergoing a
fundamental shift. It is both a shift in the shape and
organization of society and the way people find their
identity within it (postmodernity)[1] and in the paradigm or
world-view by which people make sense of society and
make their decisions within it (postmodernism).[2] 'My
thesis is that post-evangelicals are influenced by a different culture from the one which helped shape present-day
evangelicalism.'[3] This is true. But it is also true of most
other Western people today, including most evangelicals;
and evangelicalism is the growing wing of the British
Church just at this time!

The central question to be faced is how should we
respond to the emerging culture in a way which is true to
the gospel. In every era and society the Christian Church
faces the challenge of contextualization – ensuring that the
gospel is being relevantly addressed to its culture from
within, while avoiding syncretism – the cultural context
being allowed to shape the gospel to such an extent that its
costly or prophetic challenge to individuals and to society

is neutralized. To what degree is post-evangelicalism an appropriate contextual response to a new situation; the only way for its adherents to remain faithful to Christ in a changing culture? And to what extent is it syncretistic?

Before I attempt to answer that question I must challenge a major assumption of *The Post-Evangelical*.

How old is evangelicalism?

I challenge the post-evangelical identification of evangelicalism with modernity. Dave Tomlinson claims that evangelicalism and liberalism 'both find their cultural roots in modernity'.[4] As far as evangelicalism goes, that is a half-truth. The evangelical tradition was described by Max Warren as 'the whole Christian faith held in a particular balance.' The historian David Bebbington has identified four priorities that form the basis of that balance. These may be summarized as:

- a message of the necessity of personal conversion
- the Bible as the source of that message
- the cross as the heart of the message and
- activism (particularly) in spreading the message.[5]

The first three of these emphases had been continuous in the teaching of Protestant Christians since the Reformation. Number four was new. The Reformers and Puritans (with exceptions) were not really involved in cross-cultural missions, they were concerned about the reformation and renewal of the Church within Christendom. According to Bebbington, the pivotal issue which brought about change was 'a shift in the received doctrine of assurance'.[6] This came as a result of an interaction between the Reformed Protestant tradition and the emerging insights of the Enlightenment. The culture of the emerging Enlightenment era had a greater trust in the evidence of sense experience than had previously been the case. This created an environment which enabled evangelists like John Wesley and Jonathan Edwards to assure people that their experience of personal conversion was genuine. A less introspective spirituality came into being which freed converts to reach out to others. It was a move from introspection to greater assurance. The result was an extraordinary burst of creative missionary activity.

As a cultural shift from the Baroque era to the Enlightenment took place, there was an appropriate recontextualizing of Christian mission. There was no real change in the central theological convictions that marked out the magisterial reformers and their Puritan heirs from other Christians. In this sense there was strong continuity. Evangelicalism is a rooted movement whose primary doctrinal convictions far pre-date modernity. At the same time the change from one cultural era, to which biblically centred Protestant Christians both belonged and which they critiqued, to another, where a similar task was necessary, led also to a considerable degree of discontinuity in cultural ethos and missionary practice.

Evangelicalism, as we now know it, emerged as a missiological necessity. As an equal missiological necessity it brought its theological convictions with it. The crucial question concerning post-evangelicalism is whether it represents a similar missiological development as modernity fails, or whether it threatens a departure from truths far more ancient than those of the eighteenth century.

Certainty or assurance?

The Post-Evangelical focuses particularly on the evangelical concern for certainty, contrasting it with the postmodern and post-evangelical focus on ambivalence and symbolism. To a degree this makes a fair point. As the Enlightenment era developed, the Church found itself in conflict with a secular and sceptical rationalism and then with the rise of a critical biblical scholarship which often worked from sceptical presuppositions. Perhaps inevitably evangelicals tried to answer the rationalists on their own terms rather than challenging secular or sceptical rationalism itself.[7] It is easy to see this with hindsight but only as the Enlightenment era draws to a close.

However, evangelicalism also took its shape by a critical engagement with Enlightenment insights, learning to hold together the objective and subjective elements of knowing which Enlightenment thought tried to keep apart. It was assurance, aided and supported by rational thought, rather than certainty founded on rationalism, that gave evangelicalism its particular identity. Detached rationalism is discredited both from a postmodern perspective and from a biblical one, but evangelical insights about an assurance that is not anti-rational are precisely what is needed for mission to a postmodern age.

Truth and language

The most focused debate regarding post-evangelicalism, as Dave Tomlinson recognizes, is 'a difference in perception of truth'.[8] Some of his statements about the metaphorical nature of language would not cause difficulty for most evangelical scholars or college-trained clergy, and to my mind do not offer a great contrast with much of the popular evangelicalism which I know and with which I identify myself. This leads me to believe that the author's attempt to identify the cultural shape of evangelicalism may depend too heavily upon his own experience of the

New Churches and of some forms of popular charismatic piety. Equally, my own response cannot but be shaped by my experience of the Anglican (and equally charismatic) evangelicalism of the past thirty years.

Evangelicalism is not always true to itself, nor always at its best, as with every other tradition. However, my understanding of the tradition to which I belong is such that I could only place 'post' before it, by abandoning what I regard as essential insights of the gospel. Authentic evangelicalism can conform to neither modern nor postmodern conceptions of truth, even if its apologetics needs to engage with one more than the other during different cultural eras.

Dave Tomlinson proposes that we need to be 'critical realists'[9] with regard to truth. This is correct and actually represents the best of recent evangelical scholarship.[10] But what critical realism means is not so much access to truth through models or metaphors as a recognition that our capacity to know and be sure of anything is limited.

It is limited first by creation, our humanity – we can reflect upon our selves but we cannot totally step outside of our own skins, contexts or backgrounds. As Lesslie Newbigin has often pointed out, the creator did not build a spectators' gallery into the universe. Of ourselves, in contrast to the rationalistic perspective of the Enlightenment, we have no God's eye view of anything.

Second, our capacity to know is limited by our need of redemption, our fallenness; the maker's image is marred in our knowing department as everywhere else. In fact we also have a strong tendency to choose not to recognize what we do not want to know. A biblical and evangelical epistemology in a postmodern era is based on the need of revelation and redemption. It totally depends on the initiative of a God who stepped into our human context to set us free to see through his eyes. He has stepped into a world which postmodern theory has identified as one of competing small stories and given us a perspective through which we can make God's sense of the whole human story. We are realists because of revelation and self-critical of our powers of understanding and interpretation because of sin. We believe in order that we may see, and we recognize that, until Christ comes, we still need to treat our capacity for Christian understanding with a healthy degree of suspicion.

When it comes to the application of all this to biblical language, generalized statements will not do. That different parts of Scripture are written in different literary genres whose language is sometimes poetic or metaphorical is not at issue.[11] But other parts are written as history and their challenge cannot be evaded by claims about the metaphorical nature of language. Equally, the use of the metaphorical nature of language to justify a departure from the interpretation of the cross as a once and for all act of atonement in history[12] is a departure not just from evangelical theology but from traditional Christian usage. Here post-evangelical means post-biblical. Dominant theological models for the atonement do tend to arise in particular cultural eras and popular evangelical theology has focused on penal substitution, however crude or nuanced, to the neglect of others, but all models must submit to the ultimate test of Scripture.

Moving out or moving on?

None of this gives me confidence that post-evangelicals hold the key to the future shape of the Church. It is much more likely that it will be the following generation, that live beyond the 'hinge' between cultural eras; those who are growing up or coming to faith within evangelical

7

churches and who are relatively unaware of culture shift because they have only known postmodern culture, who will discover the way forward. At the moment post-evangelicalism seems too dominated by disillusion with current forms of evangelicalism to be able, as Dave Tomlinson hopes, 'to take as given many of the assumptions of evangelical faith, while at the same time moving beyond its perceived limitations'.[13] However bright a light post-evangelicalism may shine on some inadequate forms of evangelicalism, survival and recovery seem to be the prime agenda for many post-evangelicals.

Despite genuine disclaimers to the contrary, the danger is that 'post'-evangelicals quickly become 'ex'-evangelicals. The book refers to 'hundreds of people who have either moved to non-evangelical churches or who no longer attend any church at all'. At the 1996 Greenbelt Festival at least one seminar speaker spoke of being 'on the way out of evangelicalism'. There are perhaps three possible futures for post-evangelicals.

The first is simply to change from one church tradition to another. In itself this is no great issue. Christian faith is of far greater importance than any tradition within it. People are not lost to Christ by being lost to the evangelical tradition. However, the grass is not always greener on the other side and those who leave out of discomfort with evangelical culture may not necessarily find either the culture or the determining convictions of other traditions to be a more congenial home, particularly if they 'urgently need to find a fresh place for scripture in their priorities'.[14] The evidence of earlier this century is that groups like the 'liberal evangelicals' of the 1920s[15] eventually faded into the middle church mainstream rather than maintaining any significant identifiable presence or making any ongoing contribution.

A second possible outcome would be for some to depart from any recognizable form of Christianity altogether. I identify this, not to use a 'slippery slope' argument as a device to stifle necessary criticism of evangelical culture, but as a recognition of the depth of disillusion of some people within it. If post-evangelicalism is primarily a reaction against aspects of evangelicalism, the danger is that it will result in an exaggerated reaction against such primary evangelical convictions as the centrality of Scripture, while being insufficiently discriminating about other sources of spirituality. Some developments in the 'Alternative Worship' network give me cause for this sort of concern. Recent research shows that a primary reason why people leave the Church altogether, rather than move to a different tradition, is a combination of the irrelevance of the local church's activities and of the subculture in which they are carried out.[16]

As a consequence, many set out to remain Christians without any form of church affiliation. For those whose roots are deep within the Christian tradition, as many post-evangelicals are, this is a realistic possibility, although disillusion is corrosive of any spirituality. While fully acknowledging that Christianity is personal, it is also essentially corporate, both theologically and in practice. When believers lack any exposure to the Church as a learning and teaching environment, the content of their belief begins to move away from mainstream credal orthodoxy.[17] Despite popular belief to the contrary, to move out of the Church is often to move out of Christianity, for the children of the leavers if not for them themselves.

The third possibility is that post-evangelicals might pioneer new forms of church, mission and evangelism. Holy Joe's in Brixton and some expressions of Alternative Worship are precisely this and I have considerable hopes that some significant developments for the whole church will continue to come from this quarter. But other post-evangelicals appear to have reacted against evangelism itself, rather than against one particular style of it. Mission (apart from social concern) is not on their mind; escape from evangelicalism, while remaining Christian, is.

A crucial question which this chapter has been bringing into focus is, to what degree the post-evangelical reaction against evangelical culture actually disables it for Christian mission and engagement with the postmodern culture in which it is supposed to be more at home.

New worldliness for old?

Few topics are more important to post-evangelicals than the Christian's relationship with the world. The 'parallel universe' of alternativism constitutes a substantial part of what they wish to leave behind. For them feeling at home in this world is not all bad . . . Post-evangelicals also look at culture more positively.[18]

I have considerable sympathy with this statement. There are evangelical perspectives on culture which are unduly negative, or which demonize the whole of society outside of the Church, while creating a dated subculture within it which unknowingly apes many of the worst features of consumer society. These are not the only available evangelical perspectives on society, nor, in many parts of the evangelical world, are they the dominant ones, for they are biblically inadequate. It is true that where such an exclusively negative view of culture predominates, a practice of 'sanctification through withdrawal and protection' is applied.[19] But there is an equal danger that post-evangelicals are developing a naïveté about postmodern culture and that they fail to address postmodernity with the rigorous critique which they turn on evangelical culture.

The danger is of exchanging otherworldliness for assimilation, or 'new worldliness for old'. It may well be true that 'middle-class values form the dominant cultural norm in most evangelical churches',[20] but most post-evangelicalism appears to be an educated middle-class reaction to some forms of evangelicalism, despite Dave Tomlinson's impeccable working-class credentials.

Some aspects of postmodernism and postmodernity are essentially inimicable to any form of historic Christianity, others are a positive gain by contrast with modernity and Enlightenment rationalism, others still are broadly neutral, significant only to the extent that they mark a change in the missionary context. A Christian response of any substance will need to be more nuanced than that of feeling more or less 'at home'.[21]

As modernity gives way to postmodernity, Christian mission in the West faces a twin task. The task of developing a world-view from the gospel in the light of postmodern conditions and that of critiquing postmodern assumptions from the perspective of the gospel. Postmodern theory states that all knowing is perspectival, it can only be developed from context. An authentically Christian response to such a claim is first to argue from the gospel as the basis of truth without initial appeal to any other authority (e.g. reason), but then to deny the claims of postmodern relativism that seeks to restrict the authority of the gospel story to those who make it their consumer choice, or local story. The emergence of post-evangelicalism is a clear signal of the necessity of this task, but I do not as yet see signs of an insightful post-evangelical contribution to it. The need to escape the confines of the evangelical compound is in danger of clouding judgement as to the nature of postmodern life, just as much as an inappropriate and sub-biblical demonizing of the whole of culture blinds to the necessity of seeing God's handiwork in it.

If many post-evangelicals are members of a hinge generation, raised in one culture and church but young enough to feel the power of culture shift, and thus to feel deeply uncomfortable within the culture of evangelicalism, then they serve a vital function for the Church. They alert it to the profound changes which their context, cultural home and mission field are undergoing. However, those who, in one sense, are not fully at home in either world are unlikely to shape the future, any more than those conservative evangelicals whose tactic is to try to turn the clock back or simply repeat the old words and ways.

Equipped for postmodern mission

In fact, all the pieces are in place for evangelical Christianity to be a major contributor to the Church's mission in the postmodern era. The most important resources it has available include: its view of Scripture, its involvement in the Charismatic movement, its history of innovation in mission, its international networks and its growing number of committed young adults who have only ever known postmodernity.

To be an evangelical is to seek to be true to Scripture because of the conviction that to be true to Scripture is to be true to Christ. A contemporary evangelical approach to Scripture has the possibility of combining appropriate pre-modern, modern and postmodern elements.

It will be pre-modern in the sense that it submits to the will of God as revealed in the text and thus puts the human will and its capacity for detached reason or local special pleading under that authority. Underlying this is the fundamental conviction that revelation is a precondition of salvation. God must reveal himself or we cannot know our true state or destiny.

On the other hand, it will be modern in its conviction that texts which reveal the action of God in history are, by definition, open to historical investigation. Since the founding of the Biblical Research Committee of the Inter Varsity Fellowship[22] in 1938 and the opening of Tyndale House in 1944 there has been a flowering of evangelical biblical scholarship. This scholarship now shapes the syllabuses of the evangelical theological colleges, many of which train for ordination.[23]

An evangelical approach to Scripture can also be post-modern, not by accepting postmodernism's radical relativism and reduction of truth claims to power plays, but by a heightened awareness of the significance of hermeneutics and of the reader's context. Evangelical scholars like Anthony Thiselton and Kevin Vanhoozer have led the way in this field for the whole Church.

Dave Tomlinson makes the point that 'the whole centre ground of evangelicalism has become gradually charis-maticized'.[24] This is substantially true although there are strong groups within evangelicalism which are explicitly 'non' if not 'anti' charismatic. Although the point is not explicit in the book, to be post-evangelical is often to be post-charismatic, or at least post a great deal of popular charismatic piety. Again there is truth in some of the criticisms that are made. Much popular charismatic practice has tended towards dualism and triumphalism and until recently has lacked a rigorous approach to theology. On the other hand, the emergence of the Pentecostal and Charismatic movements is *the* great story of mission and church growth this century. In ninety years these movements have gone from tiny beginnings to the second largest Christian communion in the world (Pentecostalism) plus a renewal movement within every Christian tradition which equals world Pentecostalism in size. Whatever the future of Christianity and Christian mission may be in the postmodern era, it will certainly be Pentecostal or Charismatic. The move from a rather rationalistic form of Scripture-centred Christianity to a more wholistic form, equally Scripture-centred, but expecting encounters with God which engage the whole person, body, mind, emotions and spirit, is an essential missiological shift, which has happened from below, not by any Christian leader's master plan!

Furthermore, Harvey Cox, in his survey of world Pentecostalism[25] has identified it as a precursor of the emerging postmodern culture. Whatever is made of Cox's thesis, the future will include the Charismatics. This does not mean that it will be exclusively charismatic. The eclectic nature of contemporary culture makes it increasingly possible for Christians to draw from a number of previously competing sources. Andrew Walker has pointed out the need for Charismatics to develop liturgy.[26] Thanks to the writings of Richard Foster and Joyce Huggett, it is common for charismatic evangelicals to draw on the traditions of contemplative prayer. Indeed, in the report *We Believe in The Holy Spirit*[27] Sarah Coakley drew out strong parallels between praying in tongues and the contemplative tradition. Many of the students who train at Ridley Hall are evangelical charismatics with a growing love of liturgical and contemplative prayer. A spirituality for postmodernity will need to be more than charismatic, but it dare not be less.

Innovation in mission has always been a characteristic of evangelicalism. We should expect new forms of mission and evangelism to be emerging and they are. Alpha courses, seeker services, network rather than neighbour-hood-based church plants, alternative worship and youth congregations are already evident; more is surely to come. It is here, through risk and experiment together with the making of mistakes that the future shape of the Church in mission will be established. A new evangelicalism is taking shape from below.

The focus of influence within world Christianity will increasingly be the churches of the South, making the subject of this book a marginal debate. Evangelicalism is a global international movement which is well networked, but Western Christians still have little awareness how far they have moved from the centre of influence. The crucial question for all Christians at this time, evangelical or not, may be, how much can we learn from our brothers and sisters in the Two Thirds World?

In my view, the future of the Church in the West still lies substantially with the evangelicals. But there is no guarantee about the quality of that future. In a very im-portant respect the post-evangelicals are right. It will all depend on the type of evangelicalism which develops.

A positive future lies with an evangelicalism which is for the whole Church and open to learn from it, rather than existing for itself alone while being instinctively suspicious of other Christians. It is precisely this challenge to exercise responsible leadership within the whole Church which Anglican evangelicals have been struggling with in recent years.

We also need an evangelicalism which takes delight in the variety of its (denominational) traditions and roots. Evangelical unity has often been maintained at the cost of evangelical theology. Because evangelicals have united around a core of characteristic beliefs and emphases they have tended to play down the distinctive emphases of their denominations (except for arguments about baptism and church polity). But these are the points where most of us share our Christian pilgrimage with those of other traditions within our denomination. If we are Anglican, Baptist, Methodist or whatever out of biblical conviction, then our diversity, within the restraints of Scripture, becomes a crucial resource to address the postmodern delight in variety and difference, at a time of growing credal convergence in the churches, as nominal Christianity continues to decline.

This is no automatic scenario. There are real dangers of sectarianism and in-fighting. There are equal dangers of carrying on as before as though we were not all cross-cultural missionaries now. But if those most sensitive to current cultural changes do abandon the evangelical ship, a positive outcome becomes much less likely.

Post-evangelicalism is a critique of evangelicalism from its disenchanted children. There are two equal dangers, one that significant criticisms will not be taken seriously, the other that caricatures of evangelicalism and post-evangelicalism will be allowed to go unchallenged. If I am guilty of the latter, let the debate continue. For the future of the Church's mission there is urgent need of a continuing dialogue.

A dream or a nightmare?

The image which haunts me when I consider these issues is taken from C. S. Lewis's final Narnia story *The Last Battle*. As the world of Narnia ends and a new creation is born, while all kinds of people and talking beasts move 'farther in and farther up', a group of dwarves huddle together, determined not to be 'taken in'[28] by what is going on all around them. For the dwarves, more than they know, this is a nightmare. My contemporary version of this nightmare has not one but two equally determined circles of people. Both have genuine integrity and courage in their determination not to be taken in, not to be conformed to either the world or an inappropriate form of Christianity. One represents the emphasis within conservative evangelicalism that appears, without knowing it, to be trying to recreate modernity, failing to distinguish the form of Christianity within a passing cultural context, from the biblical faith itself. The other group represents many post-evangelicals. Recognizing how the world has changed, holding on to faith and finding mutual support in one another, while not really finding the way into a pattern of church for the postmodern era. The determination not to be burned again becomes too strong, a new desire for safety (one of the negative features they see in evangelicalism) keeps them away from partnership with those who might best engage postmodernity with the Gospel.

Through the wide gap between the two circles pour a whole generation of young Christians, who have never been aware of any culture other than a postmodern one. They are not a hinge generation, for they have no internal tension between the culture in which they were raised and the culture in which they now live. They are not dualist but they are passionately committed to wholistic mission. If anything, their commitment to explicit evangelism is stronger than that of their predecessors; but it is integrated with an equal commitment to justice, healing and the care of the poor and the planet. They are mostly charismatic but have a strong commitment to Scripture. They are effective in winning their friends for Christ but find it increasingly difficult to integrate them into more traditional churches;

so, with or without authority, they begin congregations of their own. This is the generation who will shape the Church for the postmodern era. I already see evidence of them at work, but much more could be to come. They are the most significant part of the next generation of evangelicals.

The gospel demands that cultural change requires each tradition within the Church to change. Because of this I am determined to keep listening to friends who identify themselves as post-evangelical, but for the sake of the whole Church I am more determined still to mentor and open the way for the new emerging breed of evangelicals.

2 The tribes of evangelicalism

PETE WARD

How do you become a post-evangelical? Suddenly whether I was, or was not, a post-evangelical was a matter of debate. Other people were talking about me, judging my post-evangelicalness. This realization came to me as I was talking with a friend who had recently joined the leadership team of an extremely large evangelical festival. 'Oh, the group have never invited you to be a speaker because they felt you were a post-evangelical,' he explained. This came as something of a shock. In the first place I have never regarded myself as being post-evangelical. More to the point I have never publicly identified myself with the term. In fact I am very clear that I have never strayed very far from a fairly standard evangelicalism (albeit with a tendency to be more 'open' than 'conservative' and with the odd charismatic twinge). Ironically I have found that my friends with a more liberal theology often regard me as something of a fundamentalist. When I added all of this up I felt a little aggrieved. How could these people whom I had never met make any kind of informed decision about what kind of evangelical I was?

I felt that I was on fairly safe ground with my evangelical commitment. I find myself to be in agreement with none other than Alister McGrath. In *A Passion for Truth* McGrath describes evangelicalism as a movement characterized by four central interacting themes:

- A focus, both devotional and theological, on the person of Jesus Christ, especially his death on the cross;
- The identification of Scripture as the ultimate authority in matters of spirituality, doctrine and ethics;
- An emphasis upon conversion or a 'new birth' as a life-changing experience;
- A concern for sharing the faith, especially through evangelism.[1]

It seems strange that it is possible to remain faithful to these central aspects of evangelical commitment and yet also be regarded as being 'post-evangelical'. Clearly perceived identity within the evangelical constituency has relatively little to do with theological issues. As McGrath points out, evangelicalism cannot just be described as a set of ideas or propositions. He makes it clear that the movement is decisively shaped by the more social forces of shifting alliances between individuals and groups. These observations lead me to reflect on what I see as the tribal nature of evangelicalism.

The evangelical tribe

My encounter with my friend is instructive in that it indicates how the social movement of evangelicalism operates. It was obvious from my conversation that to be regarded as post-evangelical was to be in some way 'beyond the pale'. Clearly some people are acceptable and kosher and some are not. There are insiders and there are outsiders. For some reason I was labelled as one of the latter. As far as I was concerned, this could not have had anything to do with doctrinal or theological issues or indeed with my own statements concerning my identity. The reason for such a distinction seemed to be based primarily upon affiliation and association. I could only assume that I was judged to be post-evangelical because of the people I knew and the events I attended. From a distance I seemed to fit the post-evangelical group better than any other. The problem with this is I am not entirely sure that there is such a gathering of post-evangelicals. I certainly don't know how to join the post-evangelical club. It seems that the group of leaders associated with the festival were primarily making the point that I did not appear to be 'one of them'. This, therefore, was a kind of kinship basis for evangelical belonging. They were sure that I was not part of their kinship network and therefore I must belong to another tribe. I could only assume that they had decided from a safe distance that I was what they called 'post-evangelical'.

My main interest in making these observations, I should point out, has nothing to do with a sense of hurt for being overlooked by this festival. I am not particularly anxious to attend any more evangelical events than I currently do. Nor am I smarting from being assessed wrongly by this group. My main reason for retelling this story is academic. This snapshot of the evangelical world reveals a social network of considerable complexity. My experience is far from being unusual. Indeed, I suspect that I was coming into contact with the way that one of the tribes within evangelicalism, albeit a particularly powerful and influential one, operated as a matter of course.

This particular tribe, I would suggest, is defined by relationship to the festival. The festival represents economic, spiritual, and social capital for the leaders of the tribe. The festival is economic capital because it is a significant moneyspinner, not simply in the charges made to those who attend, but also in the various marketing opportunities open to those able or willing to exploit the festival goer. Spiritual capital is there for the leadership because the platform of the festival presents an opportunity to exercise influence on the spirituality of a considerable number of people and churches. The festival offers social capital because participation in the leadership of the event forges friendships and alliances which otherwise may not exist. Anyone can attend the festival, but attendance, whilst it contributes to the capital associated with festival, does not bring with it automatic acceptance by the tribe. To be a full member of the tribe is to be invited to officiate at the tribal gathering in some way. At times leaders from neighbouring friendly groups may be invited to participate, but such invitations are the exception rather than the rule.

The current evangelical scene in the UK is characterized by an increasing number of tribes. Each tribe has its own organization, festival, programme or publication. Bebbington speaks of this aspect of evangelicalism as 'activism'. By this he means the tendency to be up and doing in the service of the Gospel. The proclivity to be engaged in working for the Lord has from the very earliest times led to the founding of ministries, and societies.[2] The net result of this has been that life within the evangelical movement has been decisively shaped by the activity, alliances and affiliations of individual leaders and groups, as McGrath has indicated. Evangelical identity, therefore, is to be found not only in theological agreement but also in the interplay of social relations.

Theology and social groups

Within evangelicalism doctrine is inextricably linked to social power. In *Reforming Fundamentalism* the American historian George Marsden describes the role played by

Fuller Theological Seminary and the individuals associated with it, in the evolution of a new kind of evangelical theology in the US. Central to these developments is the role played by Carl F. Henry in the editorship of *Christianity Today* and the increasing influence of Billy Graham. Henry was a lecturer at Fuller and Graham was on its Board. Marsden argues that Fuller started life within the Fundamentalist fold; however, as some of the staff began to seek a new expression of evangelical commitment, battle lines were drawn around the doctrine of Scripture. Central to this debate was the use and meaning of the term 'inerrancy' as applied to the Bible. After twenty years of protracted and vitriolic debate in which some people left the seminary and others were forced to leave, a large conference was called to attempt to lay the matter to rest. Marsden's verdict on these discussions which took place in 1965 is particularly enlightening. He points out that the theological differences between those who advocated the use of the term 'inerrancy' and those who did not was somewhat confused. On the face of it these two groups seemed to be very close in their view of Scripture. What was complicating the picture, however, was an underlying struggle between different camps within the movement. He makes it clear that

> The real issues could not be easily resolved among this large group of centerists among the new evangelicals, partly because of confusions over terminology, but mostly because the substantive question among centerists was not so much theoretical as practical: which wing of the movement did one want to be identified with?[3]

Of course for some there were real hermeneutical issues at stake, says Marsden, but for a great many the debate was not so much about the theological meaning of the term but its political usefulness. Those wishing to maintain the largely defensive stance of fundamentalism saw the term as having a usefulness in maintaining the purity of the movement. Whilst those who were less enthusiastic about its use were those evangelicals seeking to forge broader alliances with mainline denominations. For those in the middle it was a question of which of these two groups to side with.

Whilst this incident is drawn from the world of American evangelicalism, Marsden's observations are worthy of some consideration. The discussions within evangelicalism in the US over thirty years ago would seem to show that theological debate within the movement is not always what it seems. I would suggest that this may well be true whatever side of the Atlantic we are on. For the New Evangelicals of 1960s' America the term 'inerrancy' was not simply a theological phrase to describe an approach to the Bible, it was also a slogan used by particular groupings who had particular interests. It is therefore a mistake to simply treat the term as a discussion of hermeneutics alone since it is intimately related to the social relations and subculture of individual groups. What presents itself as a technical dogmatic expression is also an indicator of the style and feel of the groups within the movement. The term 'inerrancy' was clearly acting at a social symbolic as well as at a theological level.

The social nature of evangelical identity

These observations drawn from debates within American evangelicalism are pertinent because they hint at the complexity of evangelical identity and theology. The totemic functions of particular phrases and causes say as much about the tribal nature of evangelicalism as they do about the movement's beliefs. I would argue that discussions concerning the use of the term 'post-evangelical' need to be regarded in a similar light. What at first sight appears to be a discussion concerning theology carries within it a powerful energy associated with the more social nature of evangelicalism. It is probably the lack of this perspective which makes Alister McGrath's response to Dave Tomlinson's book in *Alpha* magazine somewhat inadequate.[4] McGrath, in what admittedly seems a somewhat hasty response, deals with Tomlinson solely at the level of ideas. *The Post-Evangelical* is lacking because it is ill-informed or less than well thought out in theological terms according to McGrath. At times the article feels like a pretty tough treatment of a lacklustre student's extended essay by a testy Oxford academic. It is hard to argue with the theological insights which McGrath brings to bear on Tomlinson's book. *The Post-Evangelical*, it has to be said, at a theological level is a little naïve, but for all that, McGrath seems to have missed the point. I would argue that Tomlinson's analysis of present-day evangelicalism has much to commend it not so much in the realm of theological ideas, but in its reaction to the present-day social make-up of the movement.

Tomlinson's sensibilities have emerged from his extensive involvement within charismatic evangelicalism. It is this strand of evangelicalism which has gained ascendancy in the UK in the last twenty years. Whilst acknowledging the accomplishments of these elements within the movement, Tomlinson is concerned to highlight some of the important shortcomings of this brand of evangelicalism. These include the tendency to develop what he calls a 'parallel universe' of the Christian subculture. Within this subculture Christians create imitations of things in the wider culture within which they can remain safe. The

Christian subculture, argues Tomlinson, demands that individuals conform. If they fail to toe the line they risk marginalization. At the same time, argues Tomlinson, the subculture has a definite strand of triumphalism which is a characteristic of many events and indeed festivals. Alongside this there is a defensiveness which is antagonistic towards contemporary culture.[5] These insights, whilst they carry within them theological themes, are much more to do with the style, values and attitudes of the present-day evangelical scene rather than specific theological debates. These observations by Tomlinson in *The Post-Evangelical* and in later articles contain a good deal which is true. My own work in *Growing Up Evangelical* highlights the apocalyptic tendencies in contemporary choruses, the defensiveness seen in advice given to young people and parents, and the search for safety seen in the development of Youth Ministry.[6] Of course in saying this I would argue that I am in no way identifying myself as post-evangelical (more of this later). Indeed significant criticisms of contemporary evangelicalism are being made by conservatives within the movement who are anything but post-evangelical. One example of this is David F. Wells.

Wells suggests that evangelicalism has developed three main centres since the war. These he labels as confessional, transconfessional and charismatic. The first grouping predominated on both sides of the Atlantic from the 1940s through to the 1970s. Confessional evangelicals see their identity as focused upon biblical theological thought. Their unity was based upon their shared confession of belief. In the 1970s Wells discerns a sea change within the movement. The growth and success of evangelicals have meant that the confessional emphasis based on individual founders has given way to organizational bureaucratic structures.

As a result, its outward success, coupled with its growing diversity, has redefined its center or, more precisely, relocated it. The diversity has required a shift from confessional substance to simple, organisational fraternity. This fraternity, almost by virtue of its diversity, has produced a kind of ecumenical vision in which older confessional interests have become less important and sometimes withered. The ground of relatedness among evangelicals, therefore has far less to do with living within the definitional parameters of what it meant to be evangelical and far more with belonging somewhere within the entrepreneurial or organisational life of this righteous empire.[7]

Within transconfessional evangelicalism the emphasis has moved away from doctrine towards strategy and organizational power. The emergence of the third centre, the charismatic, according to Wells has merely served to emphasize these developments considerably whilst complicating the organizational picture.

Wells's argument is that evangelicalism needs to recover its confessional roots and find its identity less in programmes and organization than in theology and biblical reflection.[8] Whilst I have some reservations concerning Wells's solutions to the current problems within evangelicalism, I am convinced that his analysis of post-war developments has much to commend it. Indeed, it would seem that the picture he paints provides an insightful backdrop to many of Tomlinson's arguments. Tomlinson's post-evangelical sensibilities, I would argue, are primarily a reaction to the emergence of organization transconfessional evangelicalism. What I have so far called tribalism is where loyalty to the festival, organization and programme is the primary indicator of identity.

Generations and cultural change
within evangelicalism

In 1990 David Neff and George Brushaber toured England researching a major feature on evangelicalism for the American magazine *Christianity Today*. They were struck by the contrasting styles and emphases in present-day evangelicalism in this country. In a passing observation they make the point that some of the divisions within evangelicalism, in particular the differences between conservative evangelicals, could well be a reflection of generational change rather than theological difference.

> The tensions between classical evangelicals and Charismatics have moderated as British Charismatics have revised their theology: experiences of the Spirit are still stressed as central, but they are not considered an essential second work of the Spirit. Nevertheless, the tensions remain visible. Perhaps it is not merely a tension between styles of worship and ministry, or between theologies, but a tension between generations ... There is an ever increasing percentage of younger evangelicals in the Church of England, but their evangelicalism is less and less like that promoted by the post war resurgence.[9]

That changes in theological emphasis and styles of spirituality may be intimately connected to the shifting sands of generational change is a major insight for understanding the tribal nature of present-day evangelicalism. This kind of analysis has been taken a little further by Steve Gerali who has examined the relationship between ecclesiology and generational values.[10] Gerali makes connections between the values of the baby-boomer generation and styles of worship. baby-boomers are those born in the United States during the 1940s and 1950s who came of age in the 1960s and 1970s. This generation, according to Gerali, share a number of characteristics. They are the 'me generation'; rugged individualists who feel that they can accomplish anything. They are upwardly mobile, corporate animals, they build empires and climb the ladder; for this group success is everything. His argument is that contemporary patterns of church life created within the USA (and I would add in the UK) reflect to a significant extent the values of this generation.

> To the baby-boomer, cultural relevance means 'trendy'. They want timely drama, contemporary light rock music, and a cadre of multi-media audio and visual experiences. In the contemporary Church, the church organ has been replaced with multi-media and icons were removed to give a worship centre the look of a theatre.[11]

Gerali's work highlights the way that contemporary styles of evangelical church life have been fashioned to suit the cultural characteristics of a particular generational group. His analysis of the US is mirrored by developments in this country during the last twenty years. What Wells has identified as transconfessional evangelicalism can be seen in the light of Gerali's work as not just the result of the growth and success of the movement. Indeed, it could be argued that the entrepreneurial style of the present-day movement is linked to the cultural values of a new generation of evangelical leaders. Thus the growth during the 1980s of New Churches, the remarkable influence of Spring Harvest, and the widespread popularity of events such as March for Jesus as well as the spread of charismatic evangelicalism in the Anglican Church, should possibly be regarded as the result of social forces within the movement as well as new theological insights and innovations. To use Gerali's terminology, these characteristics in the contemporary British scene arise from the influence of boomer, or at least boomer-like, culture.

The rise of post-war evangelicalism has been characterized by the entrepreneurial activity of a new generation of leaders. These leaders have created their own institutions and these have generated the various tribes which dot the landscape of the English religious scene. Theological debates within evangelicalism owe a good deal to the strength and influence of the various tribes which have grown up as a result of these activities. In *Growing Up Evangelical* I have tried to highlight the crucial role that youthwork has played in the formation of allegiances, theology and styles of worship. It is my view that the importance of youth camps, house parties, student ministry and festivals has been largely overlooked in theological debate concerning evangelical identity. There is a good deal of evidence that these activities have not only contributed to the growth of evangelicalism, they have also been the source of considerable diversification and tribalism. Youth activities generate followers and leaders, and they propagate shared subculture.

The post-evangelical reaction

In the US, according to Gerali, the generation to follow the boomers are referred to as 'baby busters'. Busters, also known as Generation X, are those born in the 1960s and 1970s who are coming of age in the 1980s and 1990s. This generation have a contrasting set of cultural values to that of their boomer parents. Busters are the first generation who see themselves as being less affluent than their parents. They are a consumer generation, media conscious. Most have never known life without a 'microwave, compact discs, electronic games, computer generated everything, home video entertainment and the advent of virtual reality'.[12]

> Generation Xers are anti-boomer. They do not want to be like the boomers nor do they embrace boomer values and culture. They see themselves as an alternative nation with alternative music representing alternative lifestyles. They have become content with living on less; desire more intimate relationships; are more embracing of diversity in race and gender; are more accommodating of social need; and their individual identity is not based on what they accomplish, but rather on who they are. Their definition of success is relational as opposed to financial gain.[13]

Gerali is clear that a church which has been generated by and for baby-boomers experiences problems keeping in touch with the next generation. In the UK we have experienced considerable change within the evangelical scene. Wells's insights are more than evident not only at a national level, but also in the local church. The boomer or boomer-like generation has created styles of worship and spirituality in their own image. This was the generation which inherited a prayer book from the seventeenth century, hymnody from the nineteenth century and buildings some of which have been in existence from the tenth century. The new leaders brought about change on a massive scale. The result has been developments such as the introduction of the Alternative Service Book, or new styles of music which have transformed Sunday worship, but perhaps most telling has been the approach to church buildings. Architecturally post-war evangelicalism has favoured the present day over the past and the needs of the lively congregation over the preservation of historic buildings. Thus it is this generation which has tended to dismantle the pews and replace them with plastic chairs.

The problem for the evangelicals is that we are victims of our own success. As we move towards the end of the 1990s a good many of us are starting to ask questions. Chief amongst these is the realization that the energy, vitality and creativity of the movement have created institutions and within these a subculture has thrived. It is this subculture which is now seen to be rapidly passing its sell-by date. The striving for modern worship, buildings etc. in the 1970s and 1980s has in some cases left us with a rather embarrassing legacy. Indeed, the enthusiasm for plastic chairs and functional worship spaces appears short-sighted. For the Christian young people now in their teenage years or twenties the legacy of the previous generation is increasingly experienced as embarrassing and also somewhat restrictive. The average evangelical service to young eyes can appear weary and a little bland. The point is that guitars, choruses and informality, whilst in their time being an attempt at relevance, in the 1990s appear to be yesterday's style. This style is not yet old enough to be regarded as genuine tradition. Like the faded Formica in a 1970s' kitchen it just appears sad and in need of replacement. This kind of insight, I would suggest, lies behind Tomlinson's point when he locates evangelicalism as a manifestation of modernity and post-evangelicalism to postmodernity.

> During the twentieth century evangelicalism has had to situate itself in the world of modernity, and it has had to experience and express its faith, and contend for the integrity and credibility of that faith in the cultural environment of modernity. Post-evangelicals, on the other hand, are people who relate more naturally to the world of postmodernity.[14]

Plastic chairs were modern, but unfortunately what was modern is no longer in vogue. This, in a nutshell, is the dilemma facing evangelicalism at the present time. Tomlinson is keen to point out that to be post-evangelical does not mean a retreat from key evangelical positions. At the start of his book he makes the point that to be post-evangelical is not to abandon evangelical belief as such, rather, it is to seek a way to move beyond what are its apparent limitations.[15] In this he seems to be staking a claim for a consistent evangelical position which is reforming without necessarily being liberal. Unfortunately, as McGrath so bluntly pointed out in his response in *Alpha* magazine, as Tomlinson develops his argument it is hard to escape a sense of *déjà-vu*. *The Post-Evangelical* starts with an analysis of present-day evangelicalism as a social movement, and with much of this material I find myself in substantial agreement. The problem, as I see it, is that Tomlinson quickly moves the argument onto doctrinal theological ground much of which is very reminiscent of 1960s' liberalism. It is this shift which enables McGrath to shout 'gotcha' so convincingly.

My own view is that the insights of Tomlinson and, for that matter, David Wells are extremely telling. Present-day evangelicalism has been shaped by modernity. The mistake of Wells and Tomlinson is that they seek solutions primarily at a theological level. Whilst not wanting to downplay the importance of theology, I want to argue that the more powerful area for consideration lies with evangelicalism as a social movement. Theological innovation does not happen in a vacuum. Revolutions in evangelical thinking are generated and transmitted by both charismatic individuals and by institutions. This would seem to be the chief lesson from Marsden's study of Fuller Theological Seminary. Evangelical leaders in the UK have been able to extend their influence because they have been active in building new events, festivals, youth organizations, etc. It is these activities which have produced a sense of loyalty, identity, and a shared culture for evangelicals. Whatever the shortcomings of the mainstream evangelical charismatic scene, it has to be said that it has been remarkably successful in developing tribal networks.

I have to admit that my own sense of identity as an evangelical owes a great deal to the creative activity of a previous generation of leaders. I have a sense of loyalty and a commitment to the tribe (even if others express doubts). My identity arises from my personal history of involvement in youth groups, student CUs, mission agencies and events. It is for this reason that I am enthusiastic about my evangelical identity and somewhat ambivalent about being seen as post-evangelical. The bottom line is that post-evangelicalism, if indeed it has enough substance to be labelled as an 'ism', has yet to generate itself as a significant social movement. Today post-evangelicals, as I am sure Tomlinson would admit, are far from being a recognizable tribe. To do this they will have to generate their own institutions and subcultures. It might well be that in the future the evolution of Alternative Worship and festivals such as Greenbelt may develop a distinctive tribal affiliation. If this is the case, they would secure longevity and perhaps legitimacy within the evangelical movement for post-evangelicals. If this comes about, I might find a sense of identity and group loyalty within this tribe. Until that time I find the label unconvincing and, I'm afraid to say, just a little contrived.

3 'You have to change to stay the same'

MAGGI DAWN

I read *The Post-Evangelical* when it was hot off the press in 1995. Having been involved in Holy Joe's, the group of people in South London that lived out much of the exploration of faith that Dave Tomlinson describes, I was intrigued to see what theological thought he was distilling from the whole experience. For many people, both in Holy Joe's and elsewhere, *The Post-Evangelical* gave voice to issues that were important to us: we wanted to be in communities that were genuinely and uncompromisingly Christian, but were not satisfied with being fenced in by the rules of a culture that seemed irrelevant and far removed from our world. On the other hand, we did not want the kind of artificial 'freedom' of being radical or trendy for its own sake, which is neither creative nor useful. We knew that at the heart of this was something worth saying, but as yet we were still trying to articulate it. As usual, Dave was first past the post in getting some words around the subject, and *The Post-Evangelical* was the result.

The Post-Evangelical raises some important issues that are gradually but thoroughly affecting the whole church. It does not describe a new genus of Christian, nor another denomination waiting to form, nor another theological school preparing to speak. Neither is it merely a bolt-hole for those who don't feel at home in 'normal' church. Rather, its message is that our culture is changing under our feet, and whether or not we wake up to that fact, we and our faith will be changed in any case. The question is not *whether* we will change, it's whether we will take an active and responsible part in shaping the change that is already happening.

Change is something we have to live with: it's how the world works. But I do not believe that the message of *The Post-Evangelical* necessarily implies a move away from orthodoxy. Rather, it demonstrates that to remain in continuity with orthodoxy, we have to come to terms with cultural change in order to find authentic expression of that faith. These subtleties of interpretation are slippery to define, and it is this 'same-but-different' effect that makes *The Post-Evangelical* an uncomfortable book. This is, I believe, because those who identify with its message share the experience of Topsy in *Uncle Tom's Cabin*: 'how can I know what I mean until I hear what I say?'. There is a point at which the attempt must be made to articulate one's experience. Unspoken or unexpressed thought never attains concrete reality, and it is in the process of learning how to describe and explain the idea that the idea itself takes shape. *The Post-Evangelical* is Topsy's experience for us – as it begins to give voice to what we have experienced, it helps us to understand, refine and critique that experience, and offer the wisdom of that to the wider community.

The Post-Evangelical argues for a close relationship between the message of the Gospel and the cultural medium through which it is expressed. This raises some questions. There are two extremes of thought: one is that the message and its cultural context are entirely separable – the one refers to the other. At the other extreme, reality is seen as being determined by language. Most people live as though there is some truth in both extremes. The question is, if we accept that cultural expression shapes our understanding of the gospel, can we still say that the gospel is 'true', not just 'true for me'? How do we know that we are not just making up anything we like for doctrine – constructing our own reality? Further, can we hold together the idea that the reality of God is shaped and articulated by culture and language, and the idea that God is 'other'?

My argument is that the heart of Christian experience is engagement not with words, but with The Word – God as transcendent, but met in incarnation. Language is part of the incarnational context – we are creatures for whom language is a necessary part of making real in our experience what we believe to exist in transcendence. To stay in continuity with the Christian tradition, then – to engage with the heart of what has been crystallized, reaffirmed and re-expressed through every generation of the Church – requires not merely reiteration of doctrine, but a radical reinterpretation in present-day terms. In other words, in order to stay in continuity with Christian tradition, we must also engage with the radical discontinuity of cultural expression. Meaning is not fixed, and if our religious language does not change, then far from maintaining continuity, it actually takes us away from the heart of the Christian tradition. I shall explore 'alternative' worship as an example of how interaction with culture can transform our theological understanding without cutting us adrift from our history.

Theology: 'you have to change to stay the same'

As Christians we live in dynamic tension between time and eternity, earth and heaven, concrete and transcendent.

We centre our life and faith on that which we believe to be eternal, unchanging truth. But our human condition is temporal, historically placed – we live in a world that gives us no choice about change. Biologically, culturally, temporally, everything moves and shifts constantly. Within this framework of constant change we attempt to negotiate truth which we believe to be eternal and unchangeable. Our relationship with God has to be worked out in human terms and yet not reduce God to something just like us. In other words, we have to make sense of the conflict between changing and staying the same.

In what way are we trying to stay the same? In the attempt to stay true to the roots of our faith, a mistake is often made through a lack of understanding of how to deal with our history. Feelings of staleness, boredom, and lack of relevance in our religious expression are often blamed on 'tradition', and the idea takes root that we should somehow return to the 'original' message of Christianity, shorting out 'tradition' that has supposedly fudged the issue. So the appeal is often heard for a return to 'New Testament Christianity', or for 'religion-free' Christianity. But lack of relevance, I would suggest, is not caused by what has occurred in the years between the New Testament Church and the present, but by our failure to reinterpret that tradition within the cultural context in which we find ourselves. To attempt to recreate the experience of the early Church is doubly mistaken: for a start, there is no concrete reason for believing that the early Christians' experience was qualitatively better than ours, but more importantly, it is actually impossible for us to recapture their experience. The gospel, as we know it, is thoroughly contemporary, preached to us in the context of the contemporary world, mediated through present-day culture. This is not to say that there is no such thing as transcendent truth, but to acknowledge that all of our experience is and must be articulated in the language and culture that we inhabit. To attempt to recapture the early Church experience is to create something that is true neither to their culture and time nor to ours. We cannot have a gospel untouched by tradition and culture. It is our privilege to have the faith of now, with its expression rooted in our time and place in history. For 'man's unique stand-point in history is inescapably given him in advance and helps to determine the perspective within which we have to consider God's eternal truths.'[1]

How do we deal with tradition, then? Without a doubt, tradition can set in stone deviations from the Christian message – this has been at the heart of every church split in history, from the separation of the Western Church from the East onwards. Take the example of Joseph Priestley, the most famous dissenter of the late eighteenth century, who endorsed his Unitarian view of God with the thesis that the primitive church's belief had been Unitarian and all later departures from that doctrine were corrupt. Most splinter groups and reforming movements have believed themselves to be restoring the church to the 'original' message of the gospel. But the accusation that tradition has distorted the original message must be weighed with the fact that it is also responsible for two thousand years of honing, defining, and crystallizing the faith. These are riches that we lose if we throw out tradition.

The gospel has been interpreted in countless cultural and historical settings. It is incarnated in, not superimposed on, each generation of Christians. To 'strip down' the gospel to a culture-free formula would be impossible: the only means of expression we have is the cultural framework in which we live. This does not weaken the gospel – in fact, it is part of its character. To understand that the gospel is so mediated is not to weaken it, but to accept the wonder of God's gift in Christ.

If the expression of faith changes dramatically from one cultural context to the next, though, is it really the same faith? How do we hold together cultural reinterpretation of the gospel with continuity in the Christian tradition? Nicholas Lash reminds us that 'ours is not the first social and cultural revolution in European history' and calls us back to an earlier revolution to see how the tension of continuity and discontinuity can be understood. He likens our situation to that of the sixteenth and seventeenth centuries, when faith was

> no longer able to achieve linguistic and symbolic expression in the modes inherited from the past precisely because that past ... has 'died', has become opaque and 'illegible'. Indeed, in such a situation, may it not be the case that directly and immediately to seek for an understanding of God, and thus for an appropriate mode of discourse concerning God, in continuity – in the language and form inherited from the past – would be to refuse to accept that a world had died, a culture corroded?
>
> What is the alternative? May it not be that it is precisely in the ruins of that culture, as ruins, in the 'rubble' of discerned continuities, that faith might find an appropriate mode of apprehending God, and thus might find an appropriate form of discourse concerning God? Is this redirection of faith's attention from a past rendered illegible to the wilderness of the present necessarily a rejection of the past? Or is it perhaps a hazardous attempt at fidelity? Unless a grain of wheat fall into the ground and die . . . .[2]

To insist on continuity of language and form, then, is cultural blindness – it is to refuse to accept that culture and language do change. The result is that Christianity gets stuck in a time warp, such that it not only becomes alien to those who are not part of it, but it actually changes its meaning for those who are part of it. Even if we try to maintain the cultural boundaries of the past, they will be reinterpreted by the culture that now surrounds us, such that the meaning of our faith will be changed by the very attempt to stay the same. The Amish communities of North America are an extreme example of this: their lifestyle has not made their faith stand still, it has changed its meaning. By creating a cultural time warp, they have created communities isolated from any cultural contextualization in which the meaning of words, customs and cultural icons are invested with significance they never had before. We are unavoidably connected to the culture and language of the world in which we live, and we do not have the luxury of redefining the terms unless we become a completely isolated community. As Graham Ward reminds us, 'Meaning is never fixed, never independent of histories, societies, subjectivities, the bones and sinews of language itself . . . Any mediated revelation of God must also then be historically contingent, sociologically embedded and linguistically specific.'[3]

Words and the Word

At the heart of this argument lies the fact that Christianity is not about words, it's about The Word. It is not about a static body of belief, but a living God. Statements of absolute doctrine that stand untouched and uninterpreted from one century to the next not only fail to *remain* truthful – worse, they actually *negate* the truth they once attempted to encapsulate. Religious formulae can so absorb us with a form of words that we miss the real point of the exercise. Signing 'statements of faith' supposedly demonstrates that we are true Christians, but all this actually constitutes is an assent to rational belief. Schleiermacher suggested that doctrine should be descriptive not prescriptive – rather than telling us what we ought to believe about God, it should describe what we do experience in relationship to God.[4] For all the problems this poses, it does put doctrine in perspective. A hundred years ago, F. D. Maurice lamented that 'we have been dosing our people with religion when what they want is not this but the Living God . . . We give them a stone for bread, systems for realities.'[5] The heart of our faith is not 'what' we believe, but 'who' we believe in, which makes it infinitely more worthwhile but much harder to negotiate. Doctrine and belief, of course, are important – we have to express and define what we are experiencing if it is to become real to us. But we have to take care that we do not cling to a form of words when the culture that gave them meaning has collapsed. As Tom Wright puts it, 'The Word became flesh, said St John, and the Church has turned the flesh back into words.'[6]

No formula, no statement of faith, encapsulates the exact meaning of the Gospel in such a way that is good for all times and all places. The incarnation of God in Christ is what makes God accessible to us. And as we accept our faith as incarnational, we find the way to live creatively with the tension between changing and staying the same. The Holy Spirit is the key. It is no coincidence that at the same time as our culture is recreating itself, a new flurry of interest is emerging in Trinitarian studies, and especially the role of the Spirit. The Spirit made it possible for Jesus to incarnate the truth of God at every stage in his life. Jesus' perfection was not a matter of static perfection, as if you could cut a section across his life at any point and see a perfect example of humanity. Jesus grew in obedience, not because he was previously disobedient, but because perfection is an ongoing process, not a state. It was the perfection of a work in progress, an ongoing response to the leading of the Spirit of God at every stage. A perfect apple blossom is not an apple: that doesn't make the blossom imperfect, it places it in its timescale. It is the Spirit who makes the eternal particular to each culture and generation, who enables that same truth to be incarnate in our lives.

Spirit talk is, of course, dangerous stuff. It implies risk, launching out in ways not tried before. It is not possible entirely to fence the Spirit around with fail-safe doctrines, to guarantee no heresy, to pre-empt and prevent mistakes. Life in the Spirit is a risky business simply because it is engagement with the living God. Systems and doctrines may be safer, but they are dead wood if they take priority. This is not to excuse some of the grand-scale mistakes that have been made, nor is it to blame them on the Holy Spirit. It is to be realistic about human experience: to recognize that we, with limited vision, cannot understand movements fully at their outset, and if we are not willing to take any risks at all, then we may avoid mistakes but we will also prevent grand adventures. It is a question of finding out what the tradition means for us, now. As Rahner[7] describes it, we launch out from the tradition, and we return to it. We travel the extent of its boundaries and find it is big enough to be expressed anew in the terms of our language and culture. That, of course, is why it is the tradition.

' . . . it's the way that you say it'

What is at issue, then, is not only *what* is said, but *how* it
is said. Radical reinterpretation of the gospel may give the
appearance that the very foundations of the gospel have
been upset. But the scale of change in our cultural language
is so dramatic that we cannot afford to ignore it. It runs
the whole gamut of verbal and non-verbal communication:
the way we listen, the media through which we learn, the
way information is absorbed, critiqued, interpreted and re-
expressed. Theological concerns can seem alien expressed
in new terms. To some extent it also affects our slant on
ethics, because ethical opinion is the outworking of belief
into a practical situation; thus it is when a philosophy (or
theology) meets head-on the practicalities of real life that
ethics are worked out. It looks scarily different because
the words aren't the same, the attitudes aren't the same,
and for those whose religion is firmly wedded to an
earlier cultural context, it might appear at first sight that
this is not an authentic expression of Christianity. So,
for instance, Dave Tomlinson's comments on the ideal of
family[8] seem startlingly unChristian when in fact he may
be suggesting new shapes of family or household groupings that are every bit as Christian as the ones forged in
the post-industrial age.

Fashionable? Or relevant?

In dealing with cultural interpretations of Christianity, it
is important to distinguish between being fashionable and
being relevant. There are two ways of looking at cultural
interaction with church, as we shall see below: one is to
take what we understand as 'the Gospel', and then to
dress it up in the clothes of our culture. Thus what makes
a 'youth service' different is simply a matter of style.

Culture is not so much engaged with as made use of – it's the spoonful of sugar that makes the medicine go down. But genuine cultural engagement affects your whole way of life and thought, so the message can't be separated from the medium. If we reduce this to superficial discussions of clothes and guitars, we will completely miss the point.

Fashion is often used in an attempt to make church more attractive to young people (although the problem then crops up that we can't integrate these people into 'real' church). But to be fashionable is entirely an optional extra: it has little or nothing to do with being relevant. To be relevant, on the other hand, we need both a thorough understanding of our tradition, and a genuine 'placedness' in our cultural situation. We may then simply engage with the issues of spirituality as they face us, and thus contextualize truth in the culture in which we live. As Karl Rahner reminds us, 'It is quite meaningless to want to be modern on purpose.'[9] The gospel as we know it has already been given the interpretation of a particular culture and time in history. If we accept that this is so, we are freed also to interpret it. If, on the other hand, we kid ourselves that we are not interpreting but 'staying true to the Gospel' then we are accepting uncritically a highly interpreted version of what the gospel is. Rahner's challenge is this: accept that every generation and culture interprets the gospel. And then get on with taking part in your generation's interpretation. To imagine that we can marry objective gospel truth together with a cosmetic, surface understanding of a culture is a recipe for disaster. We have to inhabit our culture (that's what being human is) to interpret the eternal truths. Michael Polanyi notes how it badly misses the point to try to dress something up in another cultural language without engaging deeply with that culture. Cultural superficiality – the attempt to short cut into a culture, using the cultural baggage to sell a message – is a lamentable mistake: it sells short both the medium and the message, misrepresenting both because the cultural icons are misunderstood and used in a shallow, confusing way.

Think of a tourist's phrase book – literal translations of some colloquial phrases demonstrates that it is worse than useless to try to translate from one language to another without any knowledge of the habits and assumptions of the culture. Language is a great deal more than vocabulary and syntax: it is a whole complex of verbal and non-verbal communication. The same thing happens if we try to make the gospel culturally relevant without allowing a deep interaction between gospel and culture. This is not to say we shouldn't try for fear of making mistakes – the only way to learn a new language and culture is to practise. But it does mean we have to take seriously the fact that our culture and language are changing, and we must allow our faith to be involved in that change if we are not to become sealed into our own little compartments.

'Alternative' worship – a way forward?

The aesthetic dimension has come sharply into focus in *The Post-Evangelical* experience, considerably affecting the slant given to theology, ethics and ecclesiology. Narrative, art, symbol, ecology and gender issues are among the concerns through which Christianity is being viewed, and the channels through which it is being imbibed. Worship and liturgy are surprising omissions from *The Post-Evangelical*, because worship speaks more clearly than anything about the way that a change in culture affects the whole experience of Christianity. Worship is the crucible where real life and experience meet theology head on.[10]

Two things happen concurrently: worshippers learn their theology through worship; they also find a place where inconsistencies between their belief and experience show up starkly, so their theology is challenged. Current moves in worship illustrate how different levels of cultural engagement can either effect a radical reinterpretation of the Gospel, or merely 'dress up' the same old fare in new clothes. The best of so-called 'alternative' worship clearly illustrates how the medium reinterprets the message – its devotees, like Topsy, are saying what they think, and in the process working out what they mean.

This was clearly visible in the recent TV series *God in the House*.[11] This series showed six services that take place in Britain, all of them dubbed 'alternative', but in fact two different approaches became obvious. In each case, lengthy footage of a typical service was broadcast together with interviews with the organizers, the speakers, readers, and musicians, and the congregation. Although all six services were considerably different from what you'd expect in the average parish church on a Sunday, only two of the services qualified as 'alternative', if by that we mean engaging at depth with cultural change. The other four were absolutely standard evangelical fare, served up in a more or less imaginative and appealing way. They featured some up-to-date musical styles: pop, rock, 'Celtic fringe' or hip-hop. The speakers and musicians were very trendy, and made an effort to be approachable and present their gospel in a user-friendly style. They went out of their way to present Jesus as 'Good News', lots of fun, not boring, deeply meaningful. But there was nothing fundamentally different about the ingredients. The services were still very much led from the front. The speakers (who were in most cases also the organizers) were invariably men, giving a homily-style, instructive talk. The relationship between

platform and congregation was very separate: all the initiative came from the platform, and the congregation
(who seemed more like an audience) were tagging along
with what happened at the front. Clearly, this was all
done with genuine sincerity and was more interesting
than some churches would be. But why call it 'alternative'? This is what youth groups and beach missions have
been doing for donkey's years. The message is the same:
it's just put across with more groovy music, clothes and
jargon.

Dramatically different, though, were the other two
services. In these two cases, the medium had changed so
much that the message had a noticeably different angle.
First, the organizers were much less visible when it actually
came to the service, giving the whole thing a much less
authoritarian feel. The voices used for readings, prayers
and so on were much more diverse: there were as many
female as male voices, to the extent that you ceased to
notice a bias one way or the other (God is not so 'male'
in this service) and the voices were coming from different
directions within the congregation ('we' are praying
together, not joining in with the platform). There was a
great deal of use of symbol, replacing words. Most notice-
able was the absence of a sermon or homily – although
what I learned from these programmes stayed with me
much longer than from the homily-style teaching. The sum
total of the symbols, the prayers, the words, and the silent
space left room for each person to grasp a clear thought
from the whole and let it sink in deeply. The symbols
used – water, earth, fire, wind – reflected the current
interest in ecological matters, and enabled people to come
to God in the context of their world. This is the God
that is in my real world, not a God I step out of my world

in order to meet. So matters of enormous importance to today's culture were quite effortlessly and unself-consciously addressed: ecology, gender, community, and so on. 'The Gospel' was being preached at both kinds of service. But the truly 'alternative' services allowed current ways of thinking and dealing with information to interact so deeply with the gospel that it was drawing out truths – ways of looking at God – that are particularly relevant to that culture.

So is the issue here about finding a more effective way of preaching the gospel to young people? Not really – if 'alternative' worship is to be of lasting value to the whole church, then it will be neither predominantly for young people, nor primarily about evangelism. A notable difference between the two types of service was that the first kind did attract a predominantly young audience: teens to thirty-somethings, but not many elderly people or young families. But the more truly 'alternative' services drew widely mixed congregations – from old to very young; fashionable and not. So this is not a phenomenon dreamed up to keep the young people happy. Second, it was not primarily an evangelistic exercise, in contrast to the first kind of service, at which the homilies were generally instructions on 'how to get saved'. So 'alternative' is not primarily about evangelism, or a precursor to 'proper church'. This last point was further illustrated by Jonny Baker (of the *Grace* service, Ealing) on Radio 4.[12] When asked if people would be attracted to this kind of service only to leave when they found out what church was really like, his reply was 'Not really: we're not doing this to try and make church more attractive, we're doing it because it's what we're like. It's to try and express our Christianity in a way that is authentic for us.'

49

At the heart of 'alternative' worship, then, is something which should not be side-lined as a 'special' activity. The principles of it could easily be incorporated into ordinary, everyday services. It is not defined by its technological trappings. The use of projectors, TV monitors, sophisticated musical production, and so on are helpful ways of engaging with a hi-tech, visually oriented culture. But the analysis above shows that it is not primarily these features that make a service 'alternative'. You can have all the technology and none of the cultural change, or you can be radically culturally transformed with a very low-tech set-up. Culturally transformed worship does not have to be expensive! This is important to register, because if 'alternative' is only possible for those with large budgets, then it is a luxury item, relevant only to those with deep pockets. Engagement with a largely visual culture is well served by TV monitors and film, but it can also be achieved with photographs cut out from newspapers, natural objects used as 'icons' or symbols, tactile items such as water or clay, and so on.

I realize that to analyse what makes 'alternative' different in this way could sound excessively critical of evangelicalism. If 'alternative' is gender-friendly, non-authoritarian and ecologically sound, does that mean that evangelicalism is authoritarian, sexist and polluting the atmosphere? Well, not exactly. It's not really a matter of 'what's wrong with evangelicalism'. My experience of Holy Joe's and other similar groups is that people very rapidly get bored with talking about what they don't like about where they came from. They are far more interested in working out how to express their Christian faith in a way that is authentic to them. They are quite happy to draw things they have learned from the evangelical world. But there is definitely something about the structures of evangelicalism that make it necessary to explain that God is *not* 'like that', as if an apology is necessary because misunderstanding is implicit in the structure. I live in a predominantly evangelical theological college, and am struck by the fact that the majority of evangelicals qualify their evangelicalism: they claim to be 'Open' evangelical, 'Liberal', 'Radical', or 'New' evangelical. Or they say, 'Well I am an evangelical, BUT . . . ' and go on to qualify what it is about evangelicalism they do or don't identify with. Clearly what is positive and helpful about evangelicalism makes people want to claim a certain allegiance, but its cultural baggage constitutes an uncomfortable subliminal message that needs explaining away. 'Alternative' worship cuts through all this: the format is non-authoritarian and gender-friendly so there's no need for the rider. Cultural shifts have radically affected the very nature of worship – right down to the way people learn, the way information and ideas are disseminated, the way power structures are shaped.

My point here is not whether these new expressions are qualitatively superior to what went before – doubtless they have a host of inadequacies of their own. The point is to try and show that what you say has everything to do with the way you say it. The relevance of the Gospel to ourselves and our friends is hampered if we constantly have to cross bridges in our minds, for instance, 'Even though this service gives the impression that God is authoritarian, male, and lives in another world from me, I know God isn't like that really.' It is more pertinent to current issues in society to say that God is gentle and humble, gives up status in favour of love, and gives 'power' a radical reinterpretation.[13] But it is not enough simply to state this. The very structure of churches and format of services has to change in order that their subliminal messages are congruent with this. The alternative scene, then, tries to voice the gospel in ways that highlight the relevance of God to our society, not just for evangelistic purposes, but for the authenticity of our own worship.[14]

Hymns ancient and postmodern

'Alternative', then, is an unfortunate cipher. First, because it implies that it is a way of doing things for those who don't want to do it in the majority (and the correct?) way. Second, because it is used, as shown above, to lump together all forms of worship that use contemporary music and modes of communication, without differentiating between levels of cultural engagement. And third, because it suggests a newness that is inappropriate. It is fascinating to notice that some of the most imaginative and fresh liturgies emerging from the 'alternative' scene are those which draw on existing liturgical patterns, reinterpreting ancient and historical forms of worship. The marrying together of 'ancient and modern' produces the kind of creative tension between continuity and discontinuity that we discussed earlier. In contrast, services or meetings that are supposedly throwing off all vestiges of tradition are far more prone to turning out the same old conservative thing – some songs, some prayers, some notices and a speaker. It seems that to be truly original (creative, fresh, innovative, relevant) you have to recreate your own history in the present. It is the relationship between the historicity and the present experience of our faith that gives it authenticity, depth and credibility. This is 'the faith of our fathers' – the faith which men and women have been living out, working out, interpreting and reinterpreting faithfully and thoughtfully over thousands of years. The way forward, both for those 'alternative' groups that feel they have lost their way, and for traditional groups that are stuck in a cultural time warp, is to engage thoroughly with the ancient tradition and reinterpret it through the culture they now live in.

This is where we came in, engaging with truth as it has been interpreted in the past; radically reinterpreting it in the modes of the present. As Nicholas Lash reminded us, there is nothing unique about a cultural revolution. But by the same token, each one *is* unique – no one has done it like *this* before. It involves commitment to something which cannot be guaranteed beforehand. Michael Polanyi draws out this idea with reference to Christopher Columbus. Columbus was not alone in thinking that the earth was round, but most people found it satisfactory, safe or convenient to live as if it was flat. Only Columbus dared to risk everything on the gut instinct that it was round. In the attempt to prove it, he did not arrive at his expected destination, but he did discover an unknown continent. 'His genius,' says Polanyi, 'lay in taking it literally and as a guide to action that the earth was round, which his contemporaries held vaguely and as a mere matter for speculation.'[15] Most people know deep down that there is more to the Christian faith than they have yet discovered, but not all are dissatisfied with where they are. *The Post-Evangelical* represents the kind of person who is not satisfied, and who sets out on a voyage of discovery to find out what else there is. There are no maps – no one has ever done it quite like this before. But it is not a question of setting out into the complete unknown. There are ways of knowing things which do not depend upon provable empirical data. Recognizing the inner knowledge that there is more, they set sail on a course to test their hunches. Like Columbus, they do not necessarily find what they thought they would. But the inner instinctive knowledge is right, and they do find undiscovered lands in the attempt to chart this new path. As Polanyi says, commitment is not possible if the object of commitment is completely known. Commitment occurs only to reality, and reality by its nature is not fully known. So our 'knowing' is a matter not of proving imponderables, but of backing a hunch.[16]

Conclusions

In conclusion, then, I believe that what _The Post-Evangelical_ has done best is open up thoughts concerning cultural movement that must in the end affect the whole church. In terms of orthodoxy, it has as much to do with continuity of tradition as it has to do with cultural change; in terms of its denominational attachment, it is going to have every bit as much effect on Catholic, Orthodox, and Liberal expressions (and any others there may be!) as it will on evangelicals. I expect the label _Post-evangelical_ will vanish as its message is absorbed. First, because its challenge is all-encompassing – it affects much more than the evangelical wing of the church. And second, because deep integration between traditional expressions of faith and cultural change of this order effects such a transformation that it is hard to trace it back to a 'mother' church. A _Post-evangelical_ person, in effect, becomes only as related to evangelicalism as she or he does to any other stream of Christianity. The degree of change is too deep to stay that close to what went before. Otherwise, we would need a whole new set of orthodoxies: Post-evangelical, Post-Catholic, Post-Orthodox, and so on.

My own experience is that when cultural change transforms one's expression of faith, it does so by opening up the breadth of Christian tradition. An initial disassociation with one's own tradition means that long-held prejudices are wiped out and the whole banquet becomes available. It was my own experience as an evangelical that 'Liberalism' and 'Catholicism' were somehow understood to be out of bounds. Once I had experienced a level of distrust of the way evangelicalism expressed my faith for me, the boundaries it set for me also became untrustworthy. The result, after a long journey around a lot of ways of thinking, is that whilst I retain a great appreciation of what evangelicalism did for me in crystallizing my faith experience in earlier years, my current experience of Christianity draws from a much wider and richer scope. I worship in an Anglo-Catholic Church, I read widely from Liberal and Catholic theological traditions, and the experience of cultural transformation has put me in touch with my religious past as well as the present. I can only regard this as a good thing. I have never been so convinced of my faith, so at ease with my self and my life, so relaxed and productive in ministry.

Because of this I find that where Dave Tomlinson recognizes a debt to evangelicalism, and wants to stay close to it theologically whilst being culturally transformed, I find the transformation more far-reaching. I think it challenges denominational and theological boundaries. Whilst reaffirming orthodoxy, new possibilities of interpretation of the Christian tradition are opened up. The sight of 'evangelical' churches practising an Anglo-Catholic liturgy suggests to me that I am not alone in this breaking down of boundaries. It is increasingly common to find cross-over between sacramental, image-symbol-based worship and more-or-less evangelical theology. An evangelical priest I met recently told me about the richly Catholic- and Orthodox-influenced liturgies they perform at his church, saying, 'I don't think those labels even matter any more. What matters is what we do now with what we've got.'

Some find that their theologies are getting a little mixed along the boundaries too – evangelicals are discovering Catholic ways of looking at things which are simply more helpful. But they don't necessarily become Anglo- or Roman Catholics (although some do). What happens is that the traditions that have been rather far apart are becoming cross-fertilized. It would be too idealistic to suppose that this was the dawning of a spontaneous ecumenical movement. But a breaking down of sharp divisions between things is now *de rigeur*: it is normal to mix and match from different sources in everything from academics to street fashion.

Whether we end up being called New evangelicals, Post-evangelicals, Radical evangelicals, Catholic evangelicals or anything else doesn't matter that much. The label game is, in any case, usually governed by those on the outside of a movement. What matters is that we are authentically Christian. What is true, good and eternal will remain. What is mistaken, cranky or irrelevant will go by the board. But whether we are closely or only indirectly affected by an 'alternative' community, the fact remains that our culture is shifting and we will either change with it or be changed by it.

4 *Living intimately with strangers – a post-evangelical pilgrimage?*

NICK MERCER

Northwest Spain was a revelation to me. As the plane circled round to land in Santiago de Compostela, I could see rolling green hills below and a landscape more reminiscent of my native Sussex than the arid desert regions of Spain, where I had stayed before in Zaragoza. The Cathedral, built over the bones of St James ('Santiago') the Apostle, dominates the old city. It has been a great place of Christian pilgrimage for a thousand years and there were many travellers there when I visited the shrine a few days later. Most of the pilgrims had walked for many miles over many days to reach their destination. They simmered on that hot August day with all the joys and weariness that a long pilgrimage brings; savouring the new friendships and shared stories; the heightened faith and sense of belonging to the Church both militant and triumphant; at best, a greater devotion to Christ for whom they had undertaken the discipline of the walk. Pilgrimage has a long and noble tradition within the Church, much neglected by Protestants because often abused by Catholics.

Some of the visitors, like me, had only flown in a few days before. They came from that part of the Christian family that does not understand pilgrimage. To them all this smacked of mumbo jumbo and salvation by works. They decided to sing some choruses in the nave and to pray 'out' the spirit of superstition that obviously pervaded a place where people genuflected, lit candles and kissed relics. An usher approached them and politely asked that they should stop singing and causing a disturbance. Vergers in Westminster Abbey would probably have done the same. Later that evening, back at the campsite, I heard some of these singers asking us to pray for the godless and misguided pilgrims. What further proof was needed of their unregenerate state, they said, than that the authorities had forbidden chorus singing in the cathedral.

Incidents like this have provoked in me an indefinable mental discomfort and pause for thought since I was a small, precocious boy in the Christian Church. In recent years I have come to understand more about myself and the Christians who have nurtured me. I have reflected on the obvious sincerity and zeal of people who seem certain that they not only have the truth, but that their way of doing the truth is superior to all others. And these people have been my friends who loved me and cared for me. Yet somehow there was often a disjunction between what we were doing and the ordinary life of my unchurched family and wider circle of friends.

I sat on the hillside overlooking Compostela, at the foot of a huge cross, and remembered some of my early attempts at evangelism as a boy of 10 or 11. On Sunday afternoons in the summer, my church held open-air services down on Shoreham beach. We would wade through the pebbles on what we judged to be the most densely populated part of the beach – always better at high tide when the masses could not spread themselves out so much – and set up a little peddle harmonium, a couple of

outdoor PA speakers, and an old valve amplifier powered
by a car battery that one of the stronger men lugged from
the road. Then we would sing songs from _100 Favourite
Hymns,_ read from the Authorized Version, share testimonies and invite the oiled and bikinied multitudes to
church that evening. My task was to go round, sweltering
in my Sunday Best collar and tie, offering people hymn
sheets in the vain hope that they might like to join in. I
tried to 'act natural' when I came across a cluster of my
school friends or neighbours. But it wasn't natural. It
was a cultural oddity, justified on theological grounds as
'preaching the Gospel'.

Ten years later at university in the early 1970s, I was
involved in _Monty Python's Flying Bible Study_ which had
at least been an 'encultured' attempt to share the Gospel,
although I realized, looking back, that it still worked on
an Us-versus-Them model of evangelism. But it was better
than the prevailing method of thrusting tracts up people's
noses, because, apparently, once a man had been converted
by having a tract nasally applied, and he had gone on to
be a famous evangelist.

Another ten years later in the 1980s, I was a Baptist
minister, sitting in a boat moored off Torquay seafront on
a Saturday evening. There was the familiar PA system, now
transistorized, but with the same old car battery – this one
with a dodgy connection which gave a surreal effect to the
voice as it ebbed and flowed on the prevailing winds:
'Welcome to the Boat Open . . . on these Satur . . . then do
take one . . . . . . joy it!' There was an accordion, a choir,
testimonies and solos, and two surly boatmen who sat like
Gog and Magog at bow and stern with mugs of tea and
fags hanging out of their mouths. One Saturday I remember the elderly speaker started off by shouting up to the
promenade: 'You may wonder what we are doing here.' I

exchanged knowing smiles with many of the youngsters sitting around me. What were we doing there?

In 1996, as an Anglo-Catholic priest, I led a pilgrimage from my parish to the Shrine of Our Lady of Walsingham. I helped sprinkle at the well, anointed with oil at the Healing Mass, and sang all thirty-seven verses of the hymn telling the Walsingham story as we processed round the garden behind the statue of Our Lady. It was a strange experience and I don't think I will ever get into the Mary thing in a big way. I had been at Spring Harvest a few weeks earlier and there were marked cultural similarities although major theological differences; and of course a lot more gin and lace in evidence – at Walsingham, that is.

These and many more are the gallimaufry of religious experiences which have shaped my life and ministry over the last forty years and I count myself lucky to have so many Christian friends who have shared with me the strengths and the weaknesses of their own traditions. I have never minded the walls of denominationalism, but I have always objected to broken glass on top of the walls. And I am but one of a growing number of Christians who have not only looked over the garden walls of very different denominations, but have walked through the gate. In a postmodern society where choice is of the essence of life, the Church is in a strong position, with fifty-seven varieties to suit most tastes and temperaments, all with one central, Christological and Trinitarian message. If only we could celebrate that diversity *and* love one another.

For me and many of my contemporaries, a dominant theme during these recent decades of social fragmentation and religious uncertainty has been integration – my life, my personality, my faith, my theology, my career, my spiritual life... And even integration of the wider Church, allowing for individual choice with conviction, yet resisting the temptation to rubbish all other positions in order to make me feel more secure in my own. This has been the growing problem of the sect-like nature of some evangelicalism and some Anglo-Catholicism. We have seen others go along a road called 'Faithful to the Tradition' and realized that for us it has become a cul-de-sac called 'The Myth of Certainty'. There are no more certainties: only reasonable grounds for confidence. This must give us a degree of humility in our walk with others of differing theological positions, and in our dealings with those struggling with faith and practice.

Good friends often see the changes we are undergoing before we notice them ourselves. I can remember the day when, walking through a little Oxfordshire village in the late 1980s, a former colleague, David Coffey, asked me if I thought I would become an Anglican, or even a Roman Catholic. I was taken aback by the seriousness of the enquiry. It had never really occurred to me to change denominations, but David obviously thought I might. Later, he explained my denominational move to others who were perplexed by what appeared so rapid a change of allegiance, in a way that helped to clarify matters for myself. He said that my theological, spiritual and career paths had converged. Let me retrace my steps along those three paths, albeit rather sketchily and sadly leaving out a number of significant people and events.

The emotional blackmail of a sound theology

As soon as I could walk, I joined my neighbours' kids at the local Baptist Sunday School. I had three, then four, then five, then six brothers and sisters and so Sunday School got you out of a crowded three-bedroomed house, both morning and afternoon in the 1950s. I liked Sunday

School: lots of friends; a colour-in book with beautiful gummed pictures to stick in each week; Sunday School anniversaries with presentation books for good attendance over the year. And many godly older men and women who loved me and gave time to me. As I grew older I joined the choir and the youth group and the Christian Endeavour and the Boys' Brigade and went to church pretty well all day on Sunday. I began to learn theology and to hear tales of liberals who dwelt beyond the Bible Belt which was the Sussex coast. Then there were the great Missionary Conventions at Holland Road, Hove, and charts of Dispensations and End Times, together with detailed models of the Tabernacle and Solomon's Temple. By my teens I was reading Scripture Union notes and IVP books and at 14 I started lay-preaching around the tin tabernacles of Sussex villages.

Church had given me the impetus to pass my 11-plus and go with my friends to High School in Worthing. It was there that I grew to love mathematics, physics and self-conscious evangelicalism under the aegis of charismatic mentors, mostly from the Brethren. Jim Gravett taught us Latin by speaking nothing but Latin when we were in class. He threw blackboard rubbers at us, kept chickens and ferrets outside his classroom and led Bible studies in the lunch hour. Taffy Evans was the headmaster who was at once fearsome and playful and who taught us Religious Instruction and muscular Christianity. Beaky Martin was a polymath who inspired me to learn about everything and who somehow taught more philosophy and theology in a maths lesson on differential calculus than I had heard in many a sermon.

The *Joy of Science* was only matched by the *Joy of Sound Theology*. (There was no *Joy of Sex* of course . . .) I was introduced to the *Banner of Truth*, to *Reformation*

Today and to the writings of Francis Schaeffer. I bought Berkhof's *Systematic Theology* and formed sound opinions on everything from women in ministry (OK as long as they weren't presiding elders) to the Established Church (some evangelicals were all right – I had been to the bastions of Broadwater, Worthing and Bishop Hannington, Hove). Once I had got the theology of the charismatic movement sorted – admittedly a trickier problem in the 1960s – I was ready for CICCU: the Cambridge Inter Collegiate Christian Union.

Cambridge was to be the finishing school of my conservative evangelical credentials, although I hung around a lot with charismatics and sang in the Selwyn Chapel choir, and this lost me serious Brownie points. To be really 'sound' you sided with John Stott rather than Martyn Lloyd-Jones; and you prayed in your college CU prayer meeting for Chapel and those who went there. You didn't attend yourself. You went to the Round Church, or to one of the Brethren halls, or joined me at Eden Strict Baptist Chapel. While studying science and the history and philosophy of science I also became a Young Earth Creationist, a position I held and championed for over ten years.

Being convinced of sound theology meant that you treated all others who claimed to be Christians but who held loose to evangelicalism as slightly suspect. Students who left CICCU to join more liberal churches and chapels were backsliders. Those who couldn't hold to the strict moral codes of evangelicalism were beyond the pale and you prayed for them with tears in your eyes. This was genuine compassion, but it was fuelled by a sectarian theology that saw all other theologies as deficient discipleship. Like all sectarian thinking, it had a powerful emotional hold on you. The intimacy of fellowship would be broken if you forsook the evangelical way. You would wander off into the relativity of liberalism if you departed in any matter from 'biblical' Christianity.

This is a hard mind set to break free of. Although I can no longer call myself a conservative evangelical, I still feel an inner pain every time I move a marker post. In 1984 I became the Laing Scholar at London Bible College and spent two years full-time, studying Genesis Chapter One. At the end of that exercise I had all but forsaken Young Earth Creationism. Eventually I realized it was only an emotional attachment and a fear of disappointing my creationist friends that made me in my dissertation *allow* for the creationist position as a possible reading of Scripture. In the course of my research I had in fact become angry at the way that Creationists (like me) manipulated the Bible and Church history to make their case. It is hardly surprising that some people find it less painful to 'give up' on Christianity altogether (although they usually haven't) rather than move away from evangelicalism to ... post-evangelicalism? In my church in Torquay we had a number of families who had been badly hurt by the Exclusive Brethren. They rarely came into church membership, because it had so many unhappy connotations, and some had a constant niggling feeling that they were bound for hell, and had forsaken the true path; the narrow way that so few enter. I understand their feelings now in a way that I could not at the time.

It is hard for exclusive theologies, and conservative evangelicalism was such in the 1960s and 1970s, to allow for a mind really open to other possibilities and points of view. Departing from the prescribed truth is too costly both in terms of inner turmoil and uneasy relationships. I know when I visit them, that *some* of my friends are praying that I will return to the truth and become an 'effective' evangelical again. How else could they pray?

A subversive spirituality

I was born at 2 a.m. one snowy Sunday, on Christmas Day, 1949. I was almost called Noel, but my parents plumped for the good Bishop of Myra, Nicholas, instead. (One of my congregation in Torquay was born exactly fifty years before me and was called Yule which made me grateful that I had not been called Holly, or even Turkey.) In a strange way, being a Christmas baby always made me feel special, and close to Jesus, the boy who shared my birthday. I never remember a time when he was not a part of my inner reality. I always spoke to Jesus and resisted any attempts to get me to 'make a decision for Christ' or to 'let Jesus into my heart' in adolescence. I was never converted. My metaphor of faith from infancy appears to have been that of evolution rather than sudden change: gradualism rather than catastrophism. Evangelicalism has been very prone to benchmark faith – conversion, baptism, backsliding, repentance, renewal, baptism in the Spirit, rededication . . . For some people this works well when set against a backcloth of progressive growth in grace. But for some who are 'forced' into this model of spiritual growth it begins to wear thin, and disillusion can set in, usually against a backcloth of increasing guilt.

There were three key elements in my early spiritual development. I grew up between the South Downs and the Channel on the banks of the River Adur. The 1950s were full of fun on beaches and in chalk pits; messing about in boats on the river; exploring in the old air-raid shelters over at the airport. Shoreham-by-Sea was a wonderful playground. Second, my father is a radio ham, so the house was always full of electrical components, tools and mechanical wonders for managing masts. I could solder soon after I could walk and blame the recent degeneration of my brain on the many electrical shocks I received in my boyhood. A third element was the beauty of music. I had a strong singing voice and very early on learnt the pleasure of making music with others in choirs and orchestras. My treble voice turned tenor by the time I was 12. By 18 I realized that male alto carried more kudos and was more marketable than an indifferent tenor. This was a decision that, somewhat surprisingly, altered the course of my life more than I could have imagined at the time.

These worlds of nature, science and music developed in me a strong sense of the power and mystery of God. Natural theology informed and gave stability to my spiritual growth, and from my twenties onwards began subtly to confuse my Christian life. My evangelical faith looked fine on paper and in the cut and thrust of student debate, but it didn't 'feel' right, or make sense of the culture in which I lived. Now I knew, of course, that I must not follow my 'feelings', those unreliable doorways to sin. I must follow my mind, that ennobled arbiter of Christian living. But even then, my reformed training reminded me of my 'total depravity' and that my reasoning too was faulty. This began to throw me back on God in a way I did not really understand at the time. I felt like John Donne:

Batter my heart, three person'd God; for, you
As yet but knocke, breathe, shine, and seeke to mend;
That I may rise, and stand, o'erthrow mee, 'and bend
Your force, to breake, blowe, burn and make me new.
I, like an usurpt towne, to'another due,
Labour to'admit you, but Oh, to no end,
Reason your viceroy in mee, mee should defend,
But is captiv'd, and proves weake or untrue.
Yet dearely'I love you, and would be lov'd faine,
But am betroth'd unto your enemie:
Divorce mee, 'untie, or break that knot againe,

Take mee to you, imprison mee, for I
Except you'enthrall mee, never shall be free,
Nor ever chast, except you ravish mee.

(Sonnet xiv)

It was all this poetry and music and liturgy and art so
closely woven into Christianity that began to produce in
me a sort of spiritual dualism. The focus of the culture
which was confusing me at this time was Selwyn College
Chapel. I had auditioned for the choir and joined the other
three male altos, who were all much better than me, but
the organ scholar desperately needed a fourth to balance
the all-male choir of about twenty voices. This introduced
me to a regime of daily Eucharists and evensongs which
was at once both utterly foreign to me and utterly com-
pelling. Furthermore, although I knew that none of the
clerics who still littered Selwyn in the 1970s were evangelicals, I realized two important things about them: they
were not lacking in the brain department and could give
good reasons for their 'middle of the road' (a pejorative
term from my background) theological positions; and they
were godly, and displayed a gentleness of spirit and devotion to God which did not fit the stereotypical picture that
countless 'sound' sermons had painted of liberals. Even
Bishop John Robinson, of the infamous *Honest to God*
debates of the 1960s, when I met him over dinner at
Selwyn was a bubbling and charming Christian man – in
favour of believers' baptism as I recall!

My chaplain, Bob Hardy (now Bishop of Lincoln), lived
next door to me on D staircase and there we had many
group discussions with the older chaplain, John Sweet, a
prayerful, caring academic with a dry sense of humour;
and with the Master of Selwyn, Owen Chadwick. He was
a powerful personality and a silent mentor for me. I would

67

often serve for him at the early morning Eucharist where he murmured the prayers by the light of the altar candles and often thrust the Gospel book towards me if the reader had not turned up – his eyesight was not up to the candlelight. I read the lesson for him at Great St Mary's, the University Church, when he was installed as Vice-Chancellor, and he took a kindly interest in my 'free church' progress after I left Selwyn.

After a difficult first term in 1969, feeling I was compromising my faith by being so involved with Chapel, I received a helpful letter from my old Worthing High School guru, Charles (Beaky) Martin. I had written to him of my concerns and he had wisely urged me to identify with 'the household of faith' in the college, even if I had some theological reservations. For the next four years, I worshipped daily in College Chapel and pedalled off after the Sung Eucharist on Sunday morning to get to Eden Strict Baptist Chapel for forty-five minutes of David Smith's great Bible exposition. Then after a very formal Sunday Evensong in Selwyn, I joined the 500-plus from CICCU at the Evangelistic Sermon in Holy Trinity. I was becoming a closet Anglo-Catholic.

My tutor at Selwyn, an engineer with a quiet devotion to Christ, always in Chapel (and now Master of Selwyn, Sir David Harrison), arranged for me to go and do my teaching practice during my fourth year at Lancing College, up the hill from my home in Shoreham. He was a governor at the school and knew that the head of physics was coming to be Schoolmaster Fellow for Easter term. It was a fantastic term, and as the Baptist Ministerial Recognition Committee for Kent and Sussex had just turned me down for training as a Baptist minister, I stayed on for two more years at Lancing. The school chapel is bigger than many cathedrals and was built as the central minster of the Woodard Foundation, an Anglo-Catholic educational trust. I was back in the choir again, deeply involved in chapel life, as well as attending my home church, Shoreham Baptist, down the hill. The 'dualism' continued and I thrived on the mystery and awe of a Sung Solemn Mass and on the intimacy and immediacy of happy clappy Bappy services.

During the late 1960s and early 1970s, I had also been deeply affected by the charismatic movement. I was at school with Stuart McAlpine and Michael Clark, and their fathers, Campbell and Dennis, and the wider circle of their friends which included Arthur Wallis, Cecil Cousen and Jean Darnall, had all made a deep impression on me. Despite the loony fringes of the movement, there was an authenticity and transparency about these men and women which again pointed me beyond the formulaic doctrines of conservative evangelicalism to the mystery of the interaction between the divine and the human – the working of the Holy Spirit. Capel Prayer and Bible weeks and the Intercessors for Britain weeks at Ashburnham Place gave me insights into prayer which I was not to come across again until I started reading some of the Fathers and Mothers of the church: Chrysostom, Francis, Hildegaard, John of the Cross, Julian, Merton . . .

I began to admit to myself, and others by my thirties, that I was theologically a Baptist, but aesthetically an Anglo-Catholic. This subversive spirituality eventually had an effect on my theology. The focus of my faith was subtly moving from 'head' to 'heart'. When I was 20, I was very secure in what I knew, but very insecure in who I was. By 40 I was very secure in who I was, but quite insecure in what I knew. There were many fuzzy edges in my faith, and the old certainties seemed naïve and unworkable. I remember standing around with half a dozen lecturers at London Bible College one afternoon discussing some particularly fundamentalist student. We had all been at Cambridge together in the 1970s. I remember commenting: 'You know, we've all become those woolly forty year olds that we despised when we were twenty!'

It was a great relief to me when I first realized that trying to get back to the fervent faith of my teens was an enormous guilt-inducing mistake. Pilgrimage requires change and if we cannot change our minds, then we cannot really change anything. I was struck by Carl Jung[1] writing on preparing people for retirement:

> We take this step with the false presupposition that our truth and ideals will serve us henceforth. But we cannot live the afternoon of life according to the programme of life's morning – for what was great in the morning will be little at evening ... I have given psychological treatment to too many people of advancing years, and have looked too often into the secret chambers of their souls not to be moved by this fundamental truth.

At the same time as all this change was going on in my spirituality/theology, my ecclesiology was also consequently undergoing a transformation. During my eleven years at LBC I realized that interpreting the Bible was a much more slippery enterprise than I had hitherto thought. And I saw that the Church played a much more determinative role in biblical hermeneutics than I had supposed. I only had to look at the way that evangelicalism had viewed the issues of divorce and the role of women, during my lifetime, to see this demonstrated. The creeds were important, for they mapped the interpretive debates of the Church. The Roman Catholic and Reformed Catholic (as some would call Anglo-Catholicism) Church had maintained credal Christianity for nearly two millennia.

I led a pilgrimage to Assisi in the late 1970s and was fascinated by all I learned of Francis. I had already met Anglican Franciscans at Lancing and at Cambridge. Then I began to read Brother Ramon's books and eventually started meeting with him. He had been a Welsh Baptist, a charismatic, and now he was a Franciscan priest – presently a solitary up at the Prayer House in Glasshampton. While still a Baptist minister I became a Third Order Franciscan. This helped to discipline my spiritual life, gave greater focus to my pilgrimage and fuelled the Spirituality courses I was teaching at LBC.

Calling or career?

Mathematics and the Baptist ministry were the competing vocations of my teens. By the time I was 17 and in the Science Sixth Form I had decided to pursue both. My teachers suggested I applied for Selwyn because it was full of ordinands and clerics who would understand someone reading Mechanical Sciences in preparation for the ministry. Cambridge has a long tradition of science and mathematics as a limbering-up exercise for the Queen of Sciences, Theology. I have never regretted the decision, although I must admit that I did a bare minimum of detailed Science while being involved in music and sport, the Christian Union and Chapel, politics and lectures by interesting people in other disciplines. These were the days of the Garden House riots, the English Faculty sit-ins, the formation of the Cambridge Students' Union (as opposed to The Union – the expensive debating society), the first mixed colleges (women were not admitted to Selwyn till 1976), charismatic splits and decimal coinage.

After two years of teaching at Lancing, I entered Spurgeon's College in 1975 to train for the ministry –

an appeal had persuaded the Ministerial Recognition Committee to (reluctantly) change its mind about my suitability. Supply teaching in Steyning Grammar School (a 2,300-pupil comprehensive school) helped me to survive financially during my four formative years at Spurgeon's. Ray Brown was the Principal. He was a church historian who also taught spirituality, both by his life and in class. He helped me to begin the integrative process between my Baptist theology and my Catholic spirituality and also made me realize that although I wanted to be a pastor, I also wanted to be a teacher and trainer.

I left to be Assistant Minister at Upton Vale Baptist Church in Torquay, where Ray had been the minister and here I experienced 'high church', pietistic, baptist worship. We had a robed choir and worked hard to give our services liturgical coherence. There was a strong brethren influence and a significant charismatic group in the church, which both served to undermine, in different ways, liturgical development, although they added much else in other areas. I had a basically Lutheran view of communion (the 'real presence' of Christ in the elements) but was aware that my congregation were essentially Zwinglians who saw the Eucharist as a memorial only (caricatured as the 'real absence').

Peter Barber was my boss for my first year. He was a Protestant Scot whom I remember saying to me as we stared at a glorious triptych behind the high altar in some cathedral: 'Doesn't it make your Protestant blood boil?' Well, no, it didn't. I had been used to gentle Cambridge Catholics and Peter's experience of Catholicism had been in Glasgow. I began to realize that temperament and formative experiences shaped your theology as much as the Bible. I could not imagine anyone who would be as good a mentor and teacher as Peter, but when he left to become General Secretary of the Scottish Baptist Union, he was followed by David Coffey who proved to be his equal as a gracious teacher and, like Peter, a man who gave me space to develop my own spirituality.

I wanted to work with students and after nearly five years at Upton Vale left to pursue research at LBC, which I knew to be a necessary preliminary for theological teaching. I began to examine my 'calling' and to sift the comments that I used to get in Torquay: 'You'll soon want your own church I suppose . . .' I didn't. I enjoyed having fingers in many pies, being a gatekeeper in so many evangelical networks, having the freedom to travel, write, teach. Furthermore, I began to understand myself as a political animal, always wanting to influence the decision-makers, always scared that I might manipulate committees rather than let decisions emerge.

When the time came for me to move on from LBC and to think about the next twenty years of my working life, I was at a loss to know what to do. I wanted to be a chaplain in an academic environment, but as a Baptist minister, such opportunities were few and far between. If only I were an Anglican, I thought . . . And then everything came together in my mind and I felt sure that this unthinkable step was indeed the next one. It was a sudden decision which I knew I must test carefully. Ramon sent me a long letter in which he showed, like David Coffey, that he knew my direction better than I did. 'It was really not "whether" but "when" you would make the change,' he wrote, and speaking of his own denominational change he said, 'I also recall that although there was a long period of inward thought and debate within my own mind and heart, yet there was a "moment" which seemed to turn the tide.'

But I was afraid that this change might be seen as a

'career move', and indeed I questioned deeply my own motivation. Was it primarily my career? Or aesthetics? Or theology? Or lifestyle? However, my two close friends David Coffey and Steve Gaukroger both encouraged me to make the move and reassured me, and my Bishop, Graham Dow, gave wise advice and direction that facilitated a smooth transition. I am now an ordained priest in the Church of England.

For many, change is often seen as weakness – Major and Blair viewed by Thatcherism and Old Labour. But 'change is the angel of a changeless God' (Archbishop Temple). The change has been a change in emphasis akin to moving from one focus of an ellipse to the other. I am more at home with the transcendent than the imminent; with mystery than explanation; with priests as the focus of the priesthood of all believers, and as a channel for transcendence, rather than ministers who equip; with paradox and uncertainty rather than closure and assurance. My earlier theology stressed beginnings – conversion; and action – busyness and behaviour, achievement and fervour. My new position embraces endings – heaven; and process – life and being, openness and reflection.

I have a long way to travel but I have good travelling companions. Relationships have been my lifeblood along the way, even when sometimes those I have intimately lived and worked with have been strangers to many areas of my interior life, as I have been to theirs. The Church is undergoing a transition that may well turn out to be a paradigm shift. Working out how we can remain faithful to the tradition and each other, while genuinely open to the Spirit's working through the Church and the Culture, takes a lifetime – and then some.

5 At root, it's a matter of the theology

MICHAEL SAWARD

When Mark Antony said that 'Brutus is an honourable man' his hearers were left in very little doubt that he thought Brutus was anything but. So, if I say that I think Dave Tomlinson is an honourable man, let's be quite clear that I mean it. I don't, in some quite important areas, happen to agree with him or think that he is right but I have no doubt that he is honest and that his intentions are entirely laudable.

He and I have both been evangelicals for most of our lives. I remain so. He now prefers to call himself a 'post-evangelical' and he does so on page 1 of his book of that title. And yet I feel an initial sympathy with his dilemma. Christopher Isherwood said, forty years ago, 'I believe in God, but I hate the sort of people who do.' I am an evangelical but I feel miles apart from many who use that title as a self-description. I have no doubt that it would have been very much to my advantage in the Church of England had I used no self-descriptive title or, indeed, any other one. To call yourself an evangelical is to invite your hearer to invent a caricature and dress you up in its clothes. It's a hiding-to-nothing epithet and people of other traditions need to know you quite well before they discover that you don't easily slip into their image of what such a prejudiced animal looks like.

So I'm not ashamed of being an evangelical because, in essence, it's a good word. To be true to such a title you have to be a 'gospel man' (which is, of course, what the word means). I hope I will never regret being a 'gospel man'. In the same way, I belong to the Church of England and I'm not ashamed of that either. But, and you can't ignore the 'but', there are plenty of facets of both the evangelical movement and the Church of England which cause considerable embarrassment. That said, and admitted, I'd still rather be both an evangelical and a Church of England man than anything else which is on offer in the Christian world.

Tomlinson and I, then, have had long-standing associations with, and commitments to, the evangelical movement. And yet. And yet. When I read his book[1] I realized that our worlds were miles apart. The kind of evangelical community in which he grew up and where, later, in adult life, he flourished, was a ghetto of constricting high walls. Take, as a few examples, the following descriptions from his book. Remember, this is his world as he himself describes it – it isn't my caricature.

> I grew up in a Brethren Church and made a personal commitment of faith as a young teenager. Some years later I received what was called the baptism of the Holy Spirit, and was subsequently asked either to renounce it, or leave the church ... I did leave and became involved in the early house church movement.

In such a congregation he encountered the attitude (in relation to another person) 'either he goes, or we do'. He discovered that such a culture 'is laden with taboos' which created 'one of the most stifling environments for creativity that I've ever known', as a friend put it. He was constricted by 'don'ts' at every point and his 'anthem' was

76

enshrined in the song 'This world is not my home, I'm just a-passing through' in which the culture outside 'was enemy territory' and his 'lurking desires' to 'enjoy some of its pleasures' were crushed under his feelings of guilt.

Tomlinson's early association with the house church movement was, in part, a reaction against this claustrophobic culture but as time has gone on he has discovered a strange mixture of the same 'closed-in' ethos coupled with a wish to be 'open' and yet not, in reality, open to ideas which pose a serious critique of his kind of evangelical experience. His kind of evangelical is still a 'packager' of the gospel, offering what he calls 'a systematised A-Z of Everything You Need to Know about Life, Death, and Eternity'. Sickened by all this, Tomlinson has said 'Auf Wiedersehen', joined the Church of England, and looks to be heading down a road which just could (though doesn't have to) lead him towards Don Cupitt and the so-called 'Sea of Faith' people, which is, of course, a reference to Matthew Arnold's *Dover Beach*, from which faith is inexorably retreating.

Reading all this, meeting and listening to him, was a reminder to me that, in the late 1940s and early 1950s, I had come across some of this in the Crusaders (to which I belonged and through which I came to faith as a teenager in 1946) and that elements of it were still around among the beleaguered Anglican evangelicals of those days. Yet, even as a theological student and ordinand, the tide of that repressed, gushy, and untheological evangelicalism was ebbing fast by the mid-1950s. I and many of my fellow-ordinands (all evangelicals) set ourselves consciously to challenge and counter it and in our curacies started to do so. 'None of that pious language of Zion' we told each other and by the early 1960s a new generation of Anglicans was growing up who were deliberately aiming to break right out of the ghetto and, in many respects, did. Our attitude to Scripture, culture, theology, and the Church propelled us well away from the more pointless taboos and set us on the road of, under God, transforming the evangelical movement in the Church of England which with no little success, we attempted in the 1960s, 1970s and 1980s. Meanwhile, the charismatic movement burst upon evangelicals with its mixture of warm spirituality at its best and idiotic fundamentalism at its worst. Sadly, just as the clearing out of the pietistic ghetto-language was beginning to take effect the charismatics flooded it all back in, especially in the individualistic world of the house churches and Tomlinson and those like him have had to react to a culture which many of us Anglican evangelicals had overturned in the 1960s.

Thus when I read Tomlinson, and listened to him, it was like plunging back into a time warp and hearing once more of the world of the hemmed-in out of which I had broken decisively (as far as I was ever in it) almost forty years ago! I suppose I have been conscious that such a world still existed as a subculture among certain kinds of evangelical (Adrian Plass has de-bunked it most effectively), but it certainly wasn't one that I lived in, or for which I felt any attraction. Quite the reverse. It is a subculture that repels me and if I felt that I would need to return to it in order to prove that I was an evangelical, then I should undoubtedly face a parting of the ways.

And of course, we're not just talking about pietistic verbiage or taboos about alcohol or dancing. We're not even talking about 'squeezing into a mould' which Tomlinson now rejects. No, we're considering a whole mind-set which crushes fun, fears sexuality, and distrusts anything and anyone whose grey-cells enjoy the challenge of a big world, big ideas, big theology, and a big, big, big

God whose world it is. Nothing more damages evangelicalism among thinking people than its fear of a wide-ranging, fully biblical, theology. Crush it all into a few neat and tidy aphorisms ('Four Spiritual Laws') as one lot claim and you can forget the complexities of life. One of the greatest curses of the kind of evangelical world against which Tomlinson has rebelled is its capacity, and often its desire, to provide simple answers to complex questions. I recall, on one occasion, gently enquiring of the pastor of one of those blockbuster American churches of ten thousand people whether or not his paperback on evangelism was just the teeniest bit too trite. He put his arm around my shoulders and said, 'Well, let's just say I like the methods I have better than the methods you don't have.' He never asked whether I had any (I actually had a section of a book of my own on that very subject), he simply justified the banality of his pre-packed approach by declining to consider even the gentlest of criticism. A, B, C. That's evangelism! You shut up!

Let's pursue some more of Tomlinson's criticisms. Again and again it is the ghetto-mindedness of his own brand of evangelicalism against which he tilts. He speaks, for example, of 'Revival' as 'a theme embedded in the evangelical psyche'. Clearly that is true of some, possibly many, in the old Brethren world. It has never been a feature of the kind of evangelicalism in which I have moved. I have always regarded it as the standard 'cop-out', the golden age supposedly once known and once more just round the corner. It's always about to burst upon us if only we would pray more, evangelize more, and so on, and so on.

Then there's the old antithesis between the 'Gospel' and the 'social Gospel'. The last time I met that in my world was in the early weeks of 1960 when my then Rector refused to support the coming Christian Aid Week because it was 'nothing to do with the Gospel'. My fellow-curate and I converted him in fifteen minutes flat. I've never come across it since.

Third, there's the suspicion of biblical scholarship, dismissively rejected as 'criticism'. 'Try talking,' says Tomlinson, 'in an average evangelical church about something like the "synoptic problem" . . . you will quickly see what I mean.' I have been a curate in two parishes and a vicar in two more and I have never been conscious of any hostility when I have mentioned such things, even in the pulpit. Indeed, I have received more favourable reaction to a series of four sermons on exactly that issue than any others in the past fory years and I was inundated later by requests from evangelical ordinands wanting copies of the series. I have (in common with many evangelicals) suggested (not dogmatized) that Jonah might well be a parable rather than a literal event. The only violent reaction I received was from the then, in the late 1960s, secretary of the Fellowship of Independent Evangelical Churches who informed me that, by believing that possibility, I could not be received in fellowship in any FIEC church. The point is that such groups (again, those among whom Tomlinson probably moved) were only at one end of the evangelical spectrum. I doubt if they have been anywhere near its mainstream, if I may be cavalier with my metaphors. What may be true is that such groups have been able to exercise an influence, far beyond their size and importance, in some of the interdenominational organizations and big conferences.

In this regard it is very interesting to compare the thrust and quality of the major platform addresses at some of the interdenominational conferences and public 'rallies' (dated word!) with those at evangelical Anglican gatherings. Chalk and cheese. The sheer competence, knowledge, and breadth of outlook exhibited at the latter by many of the speakers show the width of the gap that has opened up within the past thirty years. It is nothing whatever to do with evangelicalism or Liberalism. It is all to do with an ethos, particularly found among Anglicans, which not only permits but encourages exploratory work in field after field. One feels that here are men and women who breathe free air and aren't frightened of being shot at dawn when they challenge some very tired old 'orthodoxies' which, more often than not, were merely based on age-old repetition of hardened traditions. Once more, Tomlinson grew up in one world: I grew up in the other. He has cried 'enough' and moved on. My generation (a little older than his) didn't have to 'move out' because 'moving on' within our ethos was part of our inheritance. In one sense, we were seeing a kind of re-run of the tensions between Anglicans and Puritans of the sixteenth and seventeenth centuries. The former regarded the Bible as the 'supreme' authority, the latter as the 'sole' authority. Today, that same tension exists within the whole evangelical movement, the chief difference being that nowadays many Anglicans are so historically uninformed that they have drifted, almost unknowingly, into the 'sole' authority camp, at least as a *de facto* response.

Tomlinson feels anxiety over the way in which the adherents of the charismatic movement have, in their role as preachers, 'frequently denounced critical thinking as unbelief or as a tool of the devil'. Since he also believes (and he may well be right) that 'the whole centre ground of evangelicalism has become gradually charismaticized, adopting the style and ethos of the charismatic movement' this may well offer genuine cause for concern. Tomlinson has experienced the charismatic 'baptism of the Holy Spirit' (though he is now cautious about using that language) and

I have not (and certainly couldn't even consider using that language about the experience) but we both, I suspect, are worried about the danger of the degree of subjective pietism, exhibitionism, overconfident certainty, and lack of serious theological credibility which has dominated the movement for thirty years. Undoubtedly some of its influences (hopefully, the benign features) have percolated into the lifeblood of the new generation of leaders. Tomlinson describes them as 'charismatically inclined, if not full-blown charismatics; theologically fairly conservative; socially and politically aware; and eager to promote evangelical values within society, as well as the evangelising of individuals'. That is a very fair assessment and he cites Clive Calver, Director General of the Evangelical Alliance, as the tip of this iceberg who among others has 'quietly yet effectively taken responsibility in all quarters of the evangelical establishment'. As a result, there is a 'climate of success' in which a dynamic is generated which makes dissent very difficult indeed, and which leads to the discomfort which many evangelicals feel. He adds that, especially among charismatics, to resist the general direction in which the movement is going is perceived as resisting 'what God is doing'. Thus 'nobody dares speak up' yet 'many people who give the impression of going along with everything that is said and done actually experience all kinds of reservations, which they feel unable to voice or share with others'.

Once more Tomlinson is, I suspect, right in his assessment. I have been fortunate in having had platforms in the religious press, over the past thirty-five years, from which to offer criticism of the evangelical movement's least attractive features but I know, increasingly, that I am not now where the movement's numerical mainstream is. I believe I stand in the mainstream of the historic evangelical Anglican movement, but, once more, in numerical terms, that too is moving from its long-term moorings. Thus one is hardly ever given the opportunity to make one's case at the crucial events which mark the movement's progress (whichever way one thinks it is moving). Tomlinson's response is 'to depart and be with Post-Evangelicalism which is better'; mine is to remain and continue challenging the movement from within but conscious that, as Tomlinson puts it, resistance is 'Canute-like'. The lessons of history and theology are either ignored or rejected in a climate in which 'me and now' are supreme, in which spontaneity has overpowered continuity, in which pentecostal immediacy has quite forgotten the catholicity of tradition. This, of course, is hardly surprising since the movement's leaders are mostly baby-boomers who grew up in the 1960s and whose adult lives have been dominated by the influences of that decade. Many exciting things burst upon the world in the 1960s but we are only now discovering the impact and long-term influences which were frequently malign. In many areas of life, and certainly among evangelicals, the importance of institutions in the shaping of a community's life has been deliberately underplayed in the name of 'Spirit-filled believers' and their fellowship. Disraeli was absolutely right when he said that 'the rights and liberties of a nation can only be preserved by institutions'. He wasn't speaking of the Christian Church (but he might have been) when he added that 'it is not the spread of knowledge or march of intellect that will be found sufficient sureties for the public welfare in the crisis of a country's freedom'.

When the histories come to be written, whatever good is said about the impact on the church of so-called 'charismatic renewal' (and there has been much good to record), it seems likely that the chief defect will be the lack of understanding of, or interest in, the sustaining and developing of ongoing institutions. All too often the 1960s' children, in their charismatic form, have ignored what already exists, in favour, either of nothing with any shape, or of the need to create something new, thereby adding even more organizations to an already overcrowded market. The weakness thus exposed is possibly endemic to all evangelicals but certainly true of Charismatics. The one exception, which stands out like a lighthouse, was the voluntary decision to wind up the Fountain Trust, which was originally set up to explore the whole area of Charismatic Christian experience. Whether that brave decision ever produced the commitment to the church which was intended is another matter.

Tomlinson's conclusion, which in his book is actually his starting-point, is the conviction that 'Evangelicalism is supremely good at introducing people to faith in Christ, but distinctly unhelpful when it comes to the matter of progressing into a more "grown up" experience of faith.' By 'grown up' he means the need for mature Christians 'to desire to interact on a more positive level with theologies and perspectives which do not come from an evangelical source'. Sadly, he reflects, 'such perspectives are only ever mentioned in Evangelical circles in order to be promptly dismissed as rubbish or as a disgraceful compromise'.

Yet again we are faced with the very significant difference between the evangelical tribes. His tribal background obviously created and fostered such attitudes. Mine most certainly did not. As one who was consciously an evangelical from my late teens, I simply cannot recall any subsequent period in which I have not met with, talked with, argued with, learnt from, and occasionally collided with, those in the liberal and Catholic traditions. As a student I belonged to both the University's Christian Union and

Anglican Society. As a young curate I enjoyed the cut and thrust of post-ordination training with men right across the Anglican range. In the mid-1960s I organized a meeting wih radical Christians in South London in order to see what, if any, common ground we could discover. I twice spoke (this was unusual) at both the Christian Union and the SCM in the same universities in the same term. I worked for Christian Aid in its most radical phase. I was the first evangelical secretary of a city Council of Churches. So it has gone on. I only cite these personal instances to demonstrate that dialogue, disagreement, and friendship can easily develop where people want it and that such meetings of minds needs no loss of integrity

I should be less than honest if I pretended that such meetings have not sometimes been disappointing or that I have found some elements of the liberal–radical or the Catholic communities to be highly unattractive. Dialogue does not mean the disappearance of diversity. But then I have found aspects of certain forms of evangelicalism just as unattractive and distasteful. Unless one believes oneself to be the only totally sinless person in the gathering (and that's exactly the image that many evangelicals, wittingly or unwittingly, convey to those of other traditions), there is always something to be learnt from others.

What must already be clear is the fact that two men who have spent much of their lives accepting the same self-descriptive title, evangelical, can, when the word and its various exponents are unpacked, be discovered to have such hugely different experience of their movement

Why is this? Surely it is not difficult to trace the fact that since the days of Martin Luther (and that was the first known time that 'evangelical' was used of the reforming movement, by Sir Thomas More, in the early 1530s), the evangelical movement has taken not one, but a variety of forms. There have been evangelical Lutherans, evangelical Zwinglians, evangelical Calvinists, evangelical Anabaptists, evangelical Anglicans, evangelical Independents, evangelical Methodists, evangelical Brethren, evangelical Pentecostalists and a whole lot more. None of that lot have ever entirely agreed with each other so it is hardly surprising that those in England often fail to hold identical views.

But there is one appalling consequence. World Christianity today has approaching 25,000 Christian denominations and when Christians use the Creed and say that they believe in 'One, holy, catholic, and apostolic church', they are either forced in pretending those four adjectives are totally imprecise or that somehow something terrible has happened to the dominical prayer that 'they may all be one'. The fact which most evangelicals simply won't face up to, or even don't know, is that this vast denominational mushrooming has largely come from them. For all practical purposes it is the churches of the Reformation in general, and their descendants in the United States in particular, who have created this enormous self-generating hotch-potch, this supermarket of consumerist independency in which anyone can start up his own show at the drop of a hat. In consumerist, independency terms, it doesn't cause a qualm. The more the merrier, all competing 'in loving fellowship', to cut each other's throats right across the world. America may have contributed much to world Christianity but this is surely its most diabolically engendered legacy and I don't use the word 'diabolically' in any general sense but far more as a mark of Screwtape's activity. In 150 years, the small number of churches (already too many) have ejaculated their bastard-seed right round the globe. Did God really mean that to happen? One, holy, catholic and apostolic church? Of course most of their members aim to be good, honest, Christian men and women who merely belong to the building down the street. But those 20,000 and more denominations speak volumes when it comes to demonstrating the inability of evangelicals to have any coherent doctrine of the Church ('ecclesiology') and the consequential failure of the movement to handle matters of disagreement and difference.

Thus it is to 'ecclesiology' we have to turn because it is precisely the lack of any coherent doctrine of the Church which creates the failure of the evangelical movement to 'grow up' in the Tomlinson sense of the phrase. So what are the alternatives on offer as regards ecclesiology? There are many answers but I will confine myself to looking at three.

Before, however, I try to spell out the three options, I must look behind them to the far more fundamental question of whether the Bible offers us any kind of model. There are, of course, a whole series of metaphors. There is the body. There is the building. There is the fellowship. There is the ark. There is the bride. There is the temple. There is the flock. There is the family. Not least, there is *ecclesia*, the called-out people of God. All of these are valid, biblical images for the community of the faithful.

And yet. Long before almost all these metaphors appear in the biblical scene there is a concept introduced, so profound that it has given its very name to both elements which make up the book which we call the Bible. That concept is found long before the Jewish nation emerged from Egypt in the mighty liberation which was focused on the Exodus. One could slightly exaggerate by saying that it introduced the very idea of salvation by offering a promise to an obscure Semite, aged 75, by name Abraham, and then reiterating and developing the promise over a quarter of a century. In short, God's covenant with Abraham lies at the very heart of the story of God's saving work. The covenant is described as 'eternal' and what is promised is that Abraham will be the father of many nations and kings, who will, in him, be blessed. His descendants will be like sand on the seashore and stars in the sky.

This promise has profound implications and St Paul saw them very clearly. So in his letter to the Galatians and, in even more detail, in his letter to the Romans, he identifies the promise not just in literal physical terms, relevant only to the genetic line, but also in spiritual terms. The sons of Abraham, says Paul, are the men and women of faith who trust God's saving promise just as Abraham did long before. The covenant made with Abraham will never be withdrawn, for it is eternal. Here the contrast needs to be clearly understood when set alongside the covenant made with Moses and the Jewish nation at Sinai. That covenant is 'the old covenant' in contrast to 'the new covenant' of which Jesus spoke and with which he identified himself. Indeed, the letter to the Hebrews indicates, with absolute clarity, that the Mosaic covenant, is since the death of Christ, 'obsolete' and 'will shortly disappear'. The destruction of the Jerusalem temple and the winding-up of the sacrificial system brought that Mosaic covenant to an end.

Thus when Christians contrast 'the Old Testament' (or Covenant) and 'the New Testament' (or Covenant) they are not setting 'the front of the Bible' in contrast with 'the back of the Bible'. Many, it's true, do exactly that and their error is massive and hugely damaging to their theology. No, the contrasting 'Old' and 'New' are the Mosaic and that proclaimed by Jesus. What, however, has never been superseded or rendered obsolete, is the covenant made with Abraham which is explicitly and regularly described as 'eternal'. St Paul certainly recognized the significance of this.

The very core of the Abrahamic covenant is the creation through one man, one family, one continuous line, of a people united and held together by a promise of salvation. They are 'the church', right from Abraham's day and remain so. There is a continuity of faith and trust in a saving promise. This, of course, is a radically different view of the church than that held by those who assume that it began with its 'birthday' on the day of Pentecost, as described in Acts 2. Those who hold this latter view see a radical discontinuity with the people of the 'Old Covenant'. Those who hold the former, believe themselves linear heirs, by faith, of the ongoing eternal covenant with Abraham and also members of the 'New Covenant' which Jesus Christ provides in fulfilment of the earlier covenant with Moses which he has superseded.

So what are the consequences? The first, and perhaps, the most important, is the crucial fact that God, from the days in which he declared his great covenant promise, gave it to a community whose destiny was, like the covenant itself, announced to be 'eternal'. As the centuries rolled by, that community was given a great range of doctrinal truths to guard and, in due course, following the fulfilment of the promise in Jesus, the king, the priest, and the suffering servant, the community was widened (within the terms of the covenant) to draw in 'all the nations of the world' who were indeed to be 'blessed' by its extension to them.

Here then is the very core idea of the divine community that we now call 'the church'. By its eternal destiny its corporate nature was secured and the prayer of Jesus that it might be 'one' was the recognition of its very nature and

the need for its members to cohere within that given one-
ness.

Divisions there certainly were, but until the sixteenth
century these were relatively few. Then came the explosion
of the Reformation in Western Europe. Relatively few of
the Christian bodies which emerged were attempts to
'start again' and build 'a New Testament church'. Most
sought reformation of the Western Church, not a new
start. Certainly, in England, virtually without exception
the leaders of the Church of England believed that they
remained the historic church, purged and renewed, but
still organically linked to the apostles through the Early
Fathers and Councils.

As the centuries passed, this sense of unbroken continuity diminished and even vanished among churches which
saw their origins as rooted in some famous individual
whose name (in not a few cases) their 'church' now bore.
By the twentieth century and especially in, or stemming
from, the United States, it became increasingly common for
such churches to divide and re-divide, sometimes adding
qualifying adjectives to their title while many others simply started up from scratch at the wish of some powerful
individual or small group of enthusiasts.

Many of these groups received, or created a 'Basis of
Faith' which was aimed at holding them together. Sometimes this worked but often some specific point of doctrine
caused further division. So the groups and sects multiplied
while for the most part calling themselves 'a church'.
Some were enirely independent individual congregations,
others joined loose federations, while yet others formed
specific denominational groups.

Once again we must recall that the great majority of the
groups came from evangelical origins where the adherence
of individuals to a doctrinal basis was the ground for

'church membership'. So the Abrahamic covenant community, later defined as a 'one, holy, catholic, and apostolic church' and valuing historic continuity, usually relating to episcopal leadership, was rejected by these newer community groups who saw themselves as 'New Testament churches for believers' formed by the desire of their first generation leaders to leapfrog history and start again *de novo*.

Three major traditions will serve as an example. The Roman Catholic Church places a high value on its apostolic origins, its credal orthodoxy, and, supremely, its conviction that its guarantee of authenticity is to be found in the institution of the papacy, founded on the rock of the Apostle Peter. Accept that concept of papal authority and all else logically follows. The fact that large numbers of individual Roman Catholics, priests, theologians, and people, act as if obedience to papal authority is a matter of indifference, does not alter the reality that the whole structure of the Church depends on it.

Critics of many different kinds do not hesitate to point out that such an interpretation of the supposed Petrine foundation was held by only a very small number of the Fathers of the Church who, for the most part, believed that the 'rock' was the fact of Christ's messiahship in which Peter had declared his faith, and not Peter himself.

Whatever the truth of this, the one essential fact is that the Roman Catholic Church has to a huge extent contained its many disputing factions within the one worldwide community. In that sense, it has stood firm on the credal description of the Christian Church as 'one, holy, catholic, and apostolic'. Opponents may question its interpretation of the adjectives but they can hardly ignore the high degree of unity which holds that community together.

At the other pole are the many different Independent groups and churches. They point with pride to the fact that there have always been small groups of enthusiasts who refused to join the 'mainstream' of the historic church. Such groups were not infrequently persecuted but, despite everything, survived.

When in the sixteenth century the Bible was translated into the European vernaculars (and, especially, into English) an interesting coalescence developed. On the one hand, political radicals expressed hostility to the major churches and people read the newly printed Bibles without any benefit of scholarly interpretation and frequently treated the whole book as equally important in shaping ideas. Ignorance of historical, theological, political, and geographical background coupled with sometimes near-anarchic radical ideas led to the creation of many separate sects.

By the mid-nineteenth century evangelicals in all or most of the post-Reformation Churches felt a strong desire to find common ground and fellowship and did so by creating cross-denominational organizations with a doctrinal basis which stressed the Bible and the doctrine of justification by grace through faith. Matters concerning church, ministry, and sacraments were deliberately excluded. In this way, some of the vital elements of historic catholicity were quietly ignored. For nearly a hundred years this policy was fruitful in the development of evangelical work but in the last forty years evangelicals in the Church of England have rediscovered their inheritance, re-acknowledged their ecclesiological foundation and the old tensions have re-emerged, not least in response to both Pentecosal and 'house' churches. Whereas these latter were often founded, in England, as a deliberate response to the more traditional groups, the Anglicans were open to a range of ecumenical contacts in which the concept of a united church of 'all in each place' was running in direct contrast to an over-rigid stress on detailed doctrinal formulae. Anglicans have since the Reformation valued doctrinal statements but see their strength in the interlinking of Scripture, tradition and reason, with Scripture as the supreme (but not the sole) source of authority. Independents, and those of similar outlook, more generally treat Scripture as their only authority.

A very important consequence of all this is that the Anglicans find themselves standing between the rigidity of the Roman Catholic concept of authority and the powerful, if dissimilar, concept of Independent authority. Anglicans find a degree of freedom of ethos within their own ecclesiological tradition which does not seem to them to be so evident at either pole of the world of the other groups. Thus the issue of ecclesiology, the doctrine of the church, is becoming increasingly important in the creation of a mind-set.

This may perhaps go some way to explaining why Dave Tomlinson, the child of the 'Independency' tradition (to use a rough description) feels such a different response to his evangelical inheritance when compared with my own. What might be summed up as the 'either he goes or I do' attitude has always formed a major feature of his tradition. Holding the church together at almost all costs (short of credal heresy) is an essential element of the Abrahamic covenant type of catholicity and that is not (or does not seem ever to have been) a high priority among evangelical Independents. 'Agree with my interpretation of the Basis or get out' has again and again divided evangelical Christians even, on occasions, within the Church of England but with the rediscovery of the Anglican heritage (most visibly identified with the National

Evangelical Anglican Congress at Keele in 1967), such a tendency to split has been much less evident for a quarter of a century. Sadly, a retreat to the pre-Keele ecclesiology has emerged among some younger clergy in the 1990s, and the consequential temptation to withdraw once more into the ghetto is all too evident.

It's time to sum up. Post-evangelicalism is a response to a tradition which, despite its many strengths, has many almost endemic flaws. Since the evangelical movement iself is a coalition of a whole range of far from united 'tribes', the focus of criticism varies depending on the 'tribe' from which the critic comes. Many individual evangelicals and post-evangelicals share their distaste for some of the more banal and tasteless features which are often scum on the surface of evangelicalism's public and private life. There is not uncommonly an adolescence about evangelicalism, most particularly in its more fundamentalist outer reaches, in its tendency to ignore legitimate self-criticism, in its cult of success, in its superficial evangelism and in its cultural tastelessness.

All these are views held within the evangelical and post-evangelical communities. Some such opinions were being expressed forty years ago, especially by Anglicans, while they are only lately emerging among the more rigidly quasi-sectarian communities which have a much more marked tendency to crush such 'betrayals' in their midst.

A much more serious divide is emerging concerning the reaction of post-evangelicals to the theological, ethical, and moral issues raised by postmodernism as a secular theory. Many, and I am one, could not begin to regard the postmodern movement as one which is sympathetic to the biblical tradition. While it may offer some cogent criticisms of the secular certainties of so-called Scientific Materialism and ethical rationalism it is no more than another piglet from the litter of existentialism and the evangelical of whatever ecclesiological persuasion will need to keep his wits about him if he is effectively to disembowel this particular runt. And disembowel it he must or it will turn and rend him, trampling all over the Lord's vineyard and fouling its vintage.

6 Re-imagining evangelicalism

NIGEL WRIGHT

The debate occasioned by Dave Tomlinson's book *The Post-Evangelical*[1] is of itself sufficient evidence that he has identified a genuine phenomenon in contemporary Christianity. There are large numbers of people who have been awakened to Christ through the evangelical movement who have seemingly come to find it, at least in the form in which they have experienced it, inadequate for their continuing journey of faith. It is beyond doubt that any movement, whatever its insights and strengths, risks being undermined by its own inherent weaknesses. Tomlinson has acutely identified some of evangelicalism's weak points, especially as it is popularly expressed, and subjected them to a valuable critique. Yet the large majority of the points he has made have also been made from within evangelical ranks in some form or another by those who would gladly consider themselves continuing evangelicals. The movement is far from being without its internal conversations and self-criticisms. The most intriguing aspect of Tomlinson's book is therefore the very notion of a '*post*-evangelicalism', what it conceptually is and what it might be held to imply. Why should disillusioned evangelicals find it necessary to move to a position which, whatever the disclaimers about not being ex-evangelicals, implies moving on from or beyond evangelicalism rather than re-imagining it from within?

It so happened that prior to the publication of *The Post-Evangelical*, and in total ignorance of its imminent appearance, I was engaged in a writing project which, although very different in character, was definitely in the same ecclesiastical ball-park. *The Radical Evangelical: Seeking a Place to Stand* was published by SPCK in 1996. Although entering the market after *The Post-Evangelical* the manuscript was finished well before the latter's publication and so was not in a position to interact with its contents. Much of the impact of Tomlinson's book seems to me to reside in the title itself and once I had heard the term 'post-evangelical' for the first time I immediately understood the general mood to which it referred. Having set out some of the ways in which I would myself wish to re-imagine evangelicalism, I reflected upon the fact that in no way was I wanting to describe myself as a 'post-evangelical'. Whatever trenchant comments I might have wished to make about the evangelical faith through which I was myself won to Christ, these were comments from within, from one who recognized the strengths of what I was criticizing alongside its weaknesses. I did not, and do not, regard myself as 'post' in any sense, other than the obvious and inevitable chronological one of a position in time. That I should have failed to feel this could be, as I reflect upon it, the product of various forces. I may of course just lack imagination. I might be such a creature of confessional loyalty that I am unable to bolt from the stable in which I have found a fulfilling place of shelter. I might just be a convergent rather than a divergent thinker. Without, however, ruling out the contribution of such 'baser' factors, the higher reasons seem to me to be elsewhere.

For instance, I am aware that evangelicalism is a much more diverse coalition of theological styles, moods and convictions than external talk about 'evangelicalism' normally assumes. We are not talking about a uniform phenomenon here. I have never had much doubt therefore that within the broader parameters of a faith which has its twin foci in the normative authority of Scripture and the experience of personal conversion, the particular version of that faith which I espouse could well find a place. Furthermore, much of my own theological reflection has been inspired by a *minority* tradition within evangelicalism, Anabaptism, which has placed itself, and been placed by others, on the radical edge of Protestantism. Some of the positions Anabaptists have traditionally espoused, such as non-violence, the imitation of Christ, a Christ-centred hermeneutic and the renunciation of coercive power, have hardly commended themselves to evangelicalism at large. Yet Anabaptism was profoundly evangelical. The evangelical coalition has been able to hold together a wide variety of styles and theologies in mutual, if not unargumentative, recognition. I have been quite able therefore to hold fast to the evangelical name while constructing my own 'place to stand'.

Then again, the passage of time shows how, like most bodies of ideas, evangelicalism has changed as it has adapted itself to shifts in the wider culture. David Bebbington's standard work on the last several hundred years of British evangelical history[2] has as a basic thesis the very adaptability of the movement to Enlightenment rationalism, romanticism and expressionism in turn. Without uncritically endorsing any of these ideologies or shifts of mood, evangelicalism has transformed its own cultural expressions to take account of them. Not infrequently one hears evangelicalism being criticized precisely on account of its chameleon-like adaptability to culture. The process of adapting to the postmodern context is currently visibly under way, and perhaps Tomlinson's book is a part of it. Indeed, evangelicals are apparently far more skilful at making such cultural transitions than any other tradition in the Church, including liberalism. Even within the last thirty years there have been immense changes within evangelicalism. On the one hand, these years have seen rapid decline in Keswick-style sanctification teaching, in dispensationalism, anti-Catholicism and separatism and, on the other, marked increase in theological breadth, ecumenical commitment, the involvement of women in leadership, social awareness and political action. All this is to say nothing of the social changes which are coming to pass through the charismatic movement, the growth of black-majority churches and the new churches. Nor does it take account of the huge leaps which have been made in the growth of evangelical scholarship both at the highest levels with increasing numbers of evangelicals succeeding to professorships in theology or biblical studies and at the level of higher education with evangelical colleges enjoying increased status and achievements as well as significantly larger numbers of students. With such evidence of the ability of evangelical faith to keep pace with a fast changing society while maintaining a strong core of convictions in the process, it has seemed to me unnecessary to talk of growing beyond evangelicalism. Rather, the task is to enrich it from within, to accentuate the positive and eliminate the negative. *The Radical Evangelical* attempted to do this. This still seems to me the better approach, and with more chance of taking people along.

I have no doubt that there is an important task to be done in re-imagining evangelicalism. Such a process must happen periodically to every historic institution or tradition that wishes to renew itself in a changing world. Re-imagination should not be regarded as a superficial marketing ploy but as an intellectually serious act of self-definition. To have integrity, the process must maintain continuity with the concerns of the past while exhibiting the capacity for self-criticism. Self-criticism acknowledges that we are all limited and fallible and capable of self-improvement. We bring to the religious and theological enterprise, as to all other enterprises, our own constructions and culturally determined contributions. Yet, unlike much postmodernist and deconstructionist philosophy, re-imagining theology acknowledges there to be a core of knowledge and understanding which may be transmitted through time and which cannot be infinitely re-defined without loss. In the act of re-imagination, the content of this core is taken up into expressions of the faith which relate it more adequately to the realities of the present and suppress within it those elements which can be shown to have had negative outcomes in the past. It is not that the content itself is without negatives in the sense that it speaks words of judgement to our condition. Christians have, after all, a doctrine of sin and fall. Rather, the negatives that we have contributed and which can be seen with the perspective of time not to have served the content of faith but to have hindered it, may be suppressed or corrected in the expression of faith newly imagined. Below I shall indicate what re-imagination of evangelicalism might look like. For the moment, my concern is to argue that the concept of post-evangelicalism is not helpful to this task since it suggests convictions not so much assumed as left behind. If something has been left behind, there seems little point in seeking to re-imagine it. It is at this point that evangelicalism seems to me to delight in two strengths which the post-evangelical would be pushed to deliver. These have to do with conviction and conversion.

Dave Tomlinson freely criticizes the evangelicalism he has known on account of its apparent 'certainties'. I know exactly what he means by this in that, particularly at a popular level, the average evangelical does not easily grasp the difference between that absolute reality which is God himself and those relative expressions in which we seek to capture the truth about him, our words, liturgies and doctrines. Tomlinson's exposition of critical realism and symbolic revelation is a helpful contribution to this debate. In my experience, this is not a peculiarly evangelical problem but is found in, for instance, Roman Catholicism and some Anglo-Catholicism and within both Judaism and Islam. It would be a pity to saddle evangelicals alone on account of their new visibility with what is after all a general religious and therefore human problem, learning how to use religious language. To enable people to grasp that talk of God can be valuable and reliable and may communicate the reality of God while still falling short of being absolute is to help them make a major shift. In biblical terms, this shift is fully warranted since the Scriptures themselves distinguish clearly between the limitations of our vision and talk of God now and the perfection of our eschatological vision (1 Corinthians 13). So far so good. But I confess still to being irritated by the often-heard criticism of evangelicals on this point. The desire for certainty, we are told, is a sign of evangelicals' immaturity. It comes from their inability to cope with a world in which not everything is signed, sealed and delivered. The truly mature, we are told, thrive on mystery, ambiguity and flux. Now some of this might be true. But in addition to being highly patronizing, something evangelicals get used to since prejudice against them is one of the few respectable bigotries left, it misses the point. For one thing, there are vast numbers of evangelicals who are perfectly aware of the limitations of human formulations.

For another, if evangelicals sometimes come over as highly certain, it is rather because they are people who possess strong convictions.

To speak of 'convictions' as distinct from 'certainties', of course, immediately changes the feel of the discussion since in the current fashion to have certainties is bad but, still, to possess convictions, even burning convictions, is regarded as good. Perhaps we can see here how the process of re-imagining might work. To re-imagine certainties as convictions enables us to hold on to beliefs strongly felt while recognizing their provisional nature. It becomes impossible to criticize evangelicals for having convictions for to do so would mean critics are defining themselves as people without convictions. Here is a dilemma for post-evangelicalism, as indeed for postmodernism, in that such positions are defined not by some inherent body of ideas but by reference to convictions residing elsewhere from which those in 'post-mode' are in some sense distancing themselves by reason of disillusionment, boredom or intellectual doubt.

It is a strength of the evangelical coalition that it is one of conviction. In an age when many Christians have suffered from doctrinal heart-failure and are content to sustain themselves on a diet of minimal doctrine and maximum ritual, evangelicals, along very often with Roman Catholics although very differently from them, have persisted in being doctrinally serious, of believing in a theological authority which is mediated through Scripture. They recognize that they are set within a culture and have to bear their testimony in historical circumstances which differ from other ages. That culture has now shifted so that their presentation of the gospel of Christ must relate to postmodernity without capitulating to it as an authority equal to the gospel itself. Differing cultures have their own ways of posing questions which lead us to wonder whether the ways in which we have told the Christian story in the past belong to the essence of the story or to the contingencies of the culture in which it was told. This process of questioning belongs intrinsically to the missionary task and is a fruitful context in which the Spirit might again 'lead us into all truth', or increase our levels of insight. But at the heart of all this is the task not of assuming certain things to be true but of constantly revisiting them, wrestling with them and re-expressing them. The alternative to this is surely to become a bunch of cultural dilettantes who are merely playing a sophisticated but ultimately passionless religious game.

In this regard my hope would be that the post-evangelical mood might prove to be merely a staging-post on the journey towards the re-articulation of core Christian and evangelical convictions. Post-evangelicals might do well to ponder Paul Ricoeur's notion of the 'second naïveté'. Applied to the biblical text, this concept points out how, when the Bible is first discovered to be the Word of God, it is approached in a relatively naïve fashion. Readers ponder its texts in order to hear what God is saying to them and in their eagerness approach the text uncritically, literalistically, without subjecting it to searching analysis or questions. However, serious students who begin to approach the text critically lose their sense of wonder as they wrestle with a myriad queries in which the text is subjected to a barrage of questions. The sheer humanity of the text is exposed and the sense that it is also the Word of God disappears. God stops speaking through it. This is the point at which for many the experience of faith evaporates under the pressure of relentless questioning. But beyond the stage of criticism there is a place of 'second naïveté', of regarding and hearing the text as the Word of

God *through* its humanity and its questionableness. When readers come to this point (if they do), they may once more hear the Bible as the Word of God, and yet this time with the added insights that their critical study has added to them. The second naïveté is a desirable place to be and the staging-post of disillusionment is a necessary part of the journey towards it. This account of the matter corresponds, of course, to Dave Tomlinson's valuable exposition of 'naïve realism' and 'critical realism'. My point, however, is to apply the analysis to evangelicalism, which is also an ambiguous human reality. Any person who spends time within it will in due course become disillusioned with aspects of it and may well be tempted to reject it. But beyond the stage of disillusionment is a place of second naïveté in which without in any sense overlooking its downrightly human character (and failures), it is possible to appreciate the convictions for which it has stood and to re-imagine them in such a way as to minimize its weaknesses and maximize its strengths.

The discussion of conviction leads to a consideration of conversion. People without firm convictions are unlikely to be the means of conversion either of persons or of communities. *The Post-Evangelical* was plainly written out of a genuine pastoral concern for people who have travelled through the evangelical movement and have emerged somewhere at the other end. In this sense my own reading of the book is not that a coherent conceptual position is being advocated but that an existing constituency has been identified as a plain matter of fact. The book then seeks to help members of this constituency by engaging in certain discussions aimed at modifying or increasing understanding. What is plain, however, is that the thrust of a post-evangelical apologetic is aimed at keeping existing believers within the realm of faith rather than winning them to faith. This is a valuable and necessary exercise. What is the point of filling the bath if it is emptying just as swiftly? However, it opens up the criticism that post-evangelicalism is a form of parasite on the body evangelical, unable of itself to win converts.

Some might think this does not really matter, but I beg to disagree. I have often been struck by Sir John Seeley's comment that, 'When the power of reclaiming the lost dies out of the church then the church ceases to be the church.' Forms of Christian faith which become coy or embarrassed about conversion need to pay careful attention to themselves. Conversion is a touchstone. Christianity's astonishingly virile story from its origins in Jesus and the apostles onwards has been one of its constant ability to remake broken lives, to inspire hope and bring about personal and social transformation, and to do this in diverse culture after diverse culture. When evangelical faith is disparaged, therefore, for being good at winning people to faith but poor at helping them continue their journey, I wish to know what is wrong with alternative versions of the faith that they are so poor at persuading people to believe in the first place. When they do win people to faith it is often from a relatively sophisticated niche of the human population rather than from the masses of the ordinary. If Christianity is inherently a converting faith, what are we to say about forms of Christianity which appear to exist by *derivation* from other forms rather than by their own intrinsic vitality? And what is post-evangelicalism if not a derived form?

Clearly there is potent link between conviction and conversion. To question is a sign of maturity but to hold on to convictions in the midst of questioning is even more so. The 'paralysis of analysis' is to be avoided. People come to a change of belief and life because they encounter those who have strong convictions and are able to persuade. This is one reason why it is not enough for a theological education in the service of the church to teach people how to become critical. They also need to burn with conviction if they are to do anything other than help people embroider pre-existing, inherited beliefs. To win people to belief and faith takes the dynamic of conviction, commitment and enthusiasm. Evangelical faith deserves an honoured place precisely because it has the capacity to call people to a life-changing decision. It presents people with something that needs to be accepted or rejected but cannot just be postponed. Post-evangelicals are not theological liberals but they risk sharing with them a parasitic dependence upon a persuasive evangelicalism. It is a feature of much liberalism that it acts as a refuge for people whose initial journey to faith was enabled by evangelicals but who have turned to 'broader' understandings of religion. Some of the church's leading figures have travelled this way including such luminaries as John Habgood, David Jenkins and John Hick.

What I am contending here is not that post-evangelicals are lacking in concern about the conversion of others, although I suspect that many are if their energy is being diverted into how they can hang onto their own faith. Rather, while 'post-evangelical' is used as a self-definition it is so lame and halting a term that it can do nothing but act as an inhibitor. While people think of themselves in these terms, this can do nothing but undermine confidence in the message which is to be proclaimed or in the messengers who are to proclaim it. All the more reason then to hold fast to the name 'evangelical' and to seek to give this greater force and to elaborate upon it with increased wisdom.

Here I would wish to address the criticism that much evangelicalism is middle class and that there is a confusion between middle-class values and Christian values. It is difficult to know how to respond to this comment. It becomes so difficult to define what it means to be 'middle class' that disentangling middle-class values from Christian ones would take a great deal of discussion and self-examination. Is commitment to the sanctity of marriage, for instance, and the rejection of cohabitation, really to be defined as a middle-class value rather than a Christian one?[3] Personally, I doubt it very much. Similarly, revising the traditional Christian understanding of human sexuality is unlikely, in my opinion, to be popular with the so-called 'working classes' and is much more likely to be the preserve of *avant-garde* middle-class members of the 'knowledge élite'. What intrigues me here, however, is that from where I sit, post-evangelicalism appears to be a supremely middle-class phenomenon. The directions in which it tends are not those which the masses of ordinary people would embrace but smack of the minority cultural interests of a certain privileged sector of the middle classes themselves. The middle classes are, after all, varied and diverse. The reaction against evangelical culture has all the hallmarks of being generated by relatively sophisticated people, probably prosperous and educated beyond the average (sufficiently both to have had the opportunity to expand in various directions), who have become bored with its ambience and are searching for variety. Perhaps I am coloured here by my own encounters with people who have identified themselves to me as 'post-evangelicals'. Horny-handed children of toil they are not. I confess at this point that I am not responding to anything written in Dave Tomlinson's book but rather more subjectively to the kind of people who have come my way under the post-evangelical label. Does this therefore introduce into the discussion the whole question of snobbery? Evangelical culture, despite the claim that it is middle class, is largely generated from the grassroots, even more so since the impact of charismatic renewal. It is a folk culture, full of the good, the bad and the ugly (traits, not people). Personally, I have often tired of it, and have often been helped by it. Equally I know that were I exposed to any other cultures so much and over such a long period of time, I would tire equally of them, if not more so. I can quite understand post-evangelicals becoming bored and see only good in the search for new avenues of stimulation and inspiration. This needs to be the case and the signs are that much that is excellent is possible. Yet I am cautious of a spirit which seems unwilling to accept people in their ordinariness and which could be more concerned with what it is deriving than with what it is giving. Is this not another form of supermarket Christianity which ultimately lacks commitment not so much to the Church as a flawed cultural institution but to the people who constitute it? At the end of the day, building the church means building with bananas and there is wisdom in accepting the fact. Accepting other people for Christ's sake also means accepting, and enduring, their culture – otherwise we might be found propagating a form of élitism.

On a similar plane, the post-evangelical phenomenon is also expressed by those numbers of evangelicals who depart its ranks to gravitate to the more Catholic or Orthodox wings of the church on the grounds that they are liturgically, dramatically and visually more satisfying. There has, of course, been a beaten path in this direction from the days of Newman onwards. The curious factor here is the selective nature of the journey. There is a certain

cachet in departing evangelicalism for a more 'high culture' tradition, but those who do so seem able to turn a
blind eye to other aspects of the Catholic tradition, not
least its ritualism and hierarchicalism, which are at least
as offensive as anything found in evangelicalism.

The sum total of what I have so far written is that
whereas the post-evangelical phenomenon is a real and
challenging one, the term itself is a dead end which offers
no constructive way forward. Instead we should look to
a renewed commitment to evangelical faith and life and
should develop forms of evangelicalism which take account
of valid criticisms while maintaining continuity with the
tradition. We need to re-imagine evangelicalism. We might
be able to think in terms of 'open', 'progressive', 'constructive', 'ecumenical', 'catholic', 'unitive' or 'radical'
evangelicalism. All such terms are to be preferred to
'post'. Names are important. Content is more important
still. What might be the substance of a re-imagined evangelicalism? The rest of this chapter is devoted to this
exploration.

It has long seemed to me important that evangelicals
rid themselves of a pharisaical spirit, if by this is meant a
self-conscious pride in their own theological superiority.
As with all branches of the Church, they can be guilty of
serious sin and need to repent. Instead of seeing themselves as the remnant of the faithful Church they should
assume a more humble position within the spectrum of
theological traditions which confess the apostolic faith
as that has come to be expressed in trinitarian orthodoxy.
Evangelicalism has, by virtue of being a coalition of groupings without any shared form of ecclesiastical discipline,
erected certain symbolic doctrinal tests to determine who
is 'in' and who 'out'. The doctrines of biblical inerrancy
and penal substitution have in particular served in this

way and some would want to elevate the doctrine of the eternal, conscious torment of the impenitent in hell to this status. Attention has therefore been diverted to certain distinctives which have not necessarily been held by other persuasions in the Church, or at least not in the form recognizable to conservative evangelicals. Evangelicals have not therefore always found the common ground with others that would have enabled them to recognize them precisely as fellow-believers. This common ground is that over which the Church laboured in the first centuries of its existence and has to do with the incarnation of God in Christ and God's continuing presence with us in the Holy Spirit, all of which is signified by the doctrine of the Trinity. There are debates aplenty to be had in the Church, but that between trinitarian orthodoxy and those forms of revisionist Christianity which would depart from it is close to the heart of Christianity's identity. When it comes down to it, there is more that joins evangelical Christians to those parts of the wider Church which unambiguously confess the apostolic faith than separates them, although I for one would not wish to minimize the continuing matters at issue. Evangelical theological reflection must proceed from this essential core.

To focus here, on the vision of the Triune God, would help evangelicalism improve on some of is weaker points. Amongst these is a certain tendency so to concentrate on the world's need for redemption that there is a reduced emphasis upon the world as God's creation and gracious gift. A robust doctrine of creation helps us to live appreciatively in the world and to participate with joy in the full range of created activity. The doctrine of the Trinity affirms the origin of creation in God's creative activity, its bringing into being through the agency of the pre-existent Word of God and its sustenance and cohesion in the power of the Spirit who breathes through all creation. Creation is therefore a holy place and human beings have been set within it to engage creatively with it and to journey with creation to its ultimate goal of unity and harmony in God. None of this is to downplay the analysis of sin and fallenness which is a crucial aspect of biblical and evangelical understanding. In fact, a heightened appreciation of the world's goodness ought to lead to an equally strong grasp of the offence of human sinfulness whereby its *shalom* has been violated and vandalized. At this point the doctrine of the Trinity once more comes into play, for in summary form it attempts to do justice to the biblical narrative of God's redemptive and restoring self-involvement in the world, its suffering, pain and fallenness, in the person of Christ who is the Word of God incarnate. This is simultaneously a re-affirmation of creation, since God gladly participates in creaturehood and so sanctifies the creation, and a recognition that the way things are is not the way they should be. Yet because the one who participates in our state is the very one through whom all things have been made, what he does in sharing our life and our death has power to recreate all things. The drama of creation and redemption thus establishes that foundation upon which, without ignoring the reality of evil, the Christian can yet affirm the world's essential goodness and have hope for its ultimate transformation through the power of God active in Christ and through the Spirit.

The phenomenon of post-evangelicalism, in so far as it is currently understood and I am able to understand it, draws both from a growing tradition of theological unease concerning the adequacy of evangelical thought and life and from a social circle of people shaped by postmodernism who have come to feel that the church as it exists does not adequately minister to their needs. I have argued in this chapter that there is every reason to believe that evangelicalism can re-imagine itself both theologically, improving and strengthening its theological expressions, and socially, adapting itself in legitimate and appropriate ways to a changing culture. The term 'post-evangelical' with its inevitable associations not only of 'living after' but of 'moving on from', is therefore an unhelpful signpost. It points in a direction which is weak on the need for strong convictions and which consequently will prove ineffective in making conversions. The better way is to clarify and deepen the convictions which lie at the heart of the faith and to be renewed in the capacity to win lost people.

Notes

Chapter 1

1. See Andrew Walker, *Telling the Story*. SPCK, London, 1995.
2. See Stanley Grenz, *Primer on Postmodernism*. Eerdmans, Grand Rapids, 1996.
3. Dave Tomlinson, *The Post-Evangelical*. Triangle, London, 1995, p. 8.
4. Dave Tomlinson, *The Post-Evangelical*. Triangle, London, 1995, p. 72.
5. D. W. Bebbington, *Evangelicalism in Modern Britain*. Unwin Hyman, London, 1989, Chapter 1.
6. D. W. Bebbington, *Evangelicalism in Modern Britain*. Unwin Hyman, London, 1989, p. 42.
7. The emergence of 'Neo-Evangelicalism' in distinction to Fundamentalism in the USA during the late 1940s represents an earlier recognition of this problem.
8. Dave Tomlinson, *The Post-Evangelical*. Triangle, London, 1995, p. 90.
9. Dave Tomlinson, *The Post-Evangelical*. Triangle, London, 1995, p. 97.
10. See N. T. Wright, *The New Testament and the People of God*. SPCK, London, 1992, pp. 32–446.
11. See John Goldingay, *Models for Scripture*. Eerdmans, Grand Rapids, 1995 and Kevin Vanhoozer, 'The Semantics of Biblical Literary Forms', in D. A. Carson (ed.), *Hermeneutics, Authority and Canon*. Paternoster, Carlisle,

and John D. Woodbridge, 'God's Mighty Speech-Acts', in Philip E. Satterthwaite and David F. Wright (eds), *A Pathway into Holy Scripture*. Eerdmans, Grand Rapids.

12. Dave Tomlinson, *The Post-Evangelical*. Triangle, London, 1995, p. 100.
13. Dave Tomlinson, *The Post-Evangelical*. Triangle, London, 1995, p. 7.
14. Dave Tomlinson, *The Post-Evangelical*. Triangle, London, 1995, p. 105.
15. For background see Kenneth Hylson-Smith, *Evangelical in the Church of England 1734–1984*. T. & T. Clark, Edinburgh, 1988, pp. 246–55.
16. Michael Fanstone, *The Sheep that Got Away: Why do People Leave the Church?* Monarch, Eastbourne, 1993, Chapter 7.
17. See Grace Davie, *Religion in Britain: Believing Without Belonging*. Blackwell, Oxford, 1994, Chapters 5–7.
18. Dave Tomlinson, *The Post-Evangelical*. Triangle, London, 1995, p. 125.
19. See Pete Ward, *Growing Up Evangelical*. SPCK, London, 1996, Part 3.
20. Dave Tomlinson, *The Post-Evangelical*. Triangle, London, 1995, p. 32.
21. For two nuanced evangelical responses see J. Richard Middleton and Brian J. Walsh, *Truth is Stranger than it Used to Be*. SPCK, London, 1995 and A. Thiselton, *Interpreting God and the Postmodern Self*. T. & T. Clark, Edinburgh, 1995.
22. Now the Universities and Colleges Christian Fellowship.
23. My own view is that if this sort of relevant scholarship had been more often translated into evangelical pulpits, some aspects of *The Post-Evangelical* would never have been written.
24. Dave Tomlinson, *The Post-Evangelical*. Triangle, London, 1995, p. 15.
25. Harvey Cox, *Fire From Heaven*. Cassell, London, 1996.
26. Andrew Walker, *Telling the Story*. SPCK, London, 1995.

27. Church of England Doctrine Commission, Church House Publishing, London, 1991, Chapter 2.
28. See C. S. Lewis, *The Last Battle*. 1956.

Chapter 2

1. Alister E. McGrath, *A Passion for Truth*. Apollos, Leicester, 1996, p. 22.
2. D. W. Bebbington, *Evangelicalism in Modern Britain*. Unwin Hyman, London, 1989, pp. 10–12.
3. George M. Marsden, *Reforming Fundamentalism*. Eerdmans, Grand Rapids, 1987, p. 229.
4. Alister McGrath, 'Prophets of Doubt', *Alpha*, August 1996.
5. D. Tomlinson, 'Heralds of Hope', *Alpha*, September 1996.
6. See Pete Ward, *Growing Up Evangelical*. SPCK, London, 1996.
7. David F. Wells, 'On Being Evangelical: Some Theological Differences and Similarities', in M. Noll, D. W. Bebbington and G. A. Rawlyk (eds), *Evangelicalism*. OUP, Oxford, 1994, p. 391.
8. See David F. Wells, *No Place for Truth*. IVP, Leicester, 1993.
9. David Neff and George K. Brushaber, 'The Remaking of English Evangelicalism', *Christianity Today*, February 1990.
10. Steve Gerali, 'Paradigms in Contemporary Church which Reflect Generational Values', in Pete Ward (ed.), *The Church and Youth Ministry*. Lynx, Oxford, 1995.
11. Steve Gerali, 'Paradigms in Contemporary Church which Reflect Generational Values', p. 55.
12. Steve Gerali, 'Paradigms in Contemporary Church which Reflect Generational Values', p. 54.
13. Steve Gerali, 'Paradigms in Contemporary Church which Reflect Generational Values', p. 54.
14. Dave Tomlinson, *The Post-Evangelical*. Triangle, London, 1995, p. 8.

15. Dave Tomlinson, *The Post-Evangelical*. Triangle, London, 1995, p. 7.

Chapter 3

1. Karl Rahner, *Theological Investigations*. vol. 1, tr. C. Ernst, O.P., London, 1961, 1965, p. 153.
2. N. Lash, *Theology on Dover Beach*. DLT, London, 1979, p. 41.
3. G. Ward, 'Theological Materialism' in C. Crowder (ed.), *God and Reality*. Mowbray, London, 1997, p. 146.
4. F. Schleiermacher, *The Christian Faith*. 1928, pp. 740–1.
5. F. D. Maurice, *Life of F. D. Maurice Chiefly Told in his Own Letters* vol. 1, ed. Frederick Maurice, 1885, p. 369.
6. Tom Wright, *The Crown and the Fire*. SPCK, London, 1992, p. 51.
7. Karl Rahner, *Foundations of Christian Faith*. tr. W. Dych, DLT, London, 1978.
8. Dave Tomlinson, *The Post-Evangelical*. Triangle, London, 1995, pp. 34–9.
9. Karl Rahner, *Theological Investigations*. vol. 1, tr. C. Ernst, O.P., London, 1961, 1965, p. 153.
10. J. D. Crichton, 'A Theology of Worship', in C. Jones, G. Wainwright *et al.* (eds), *The Study of Liturgy*. 2nd edn, SPCK, London, 1992, pp. 7–9.
11. Channel 4, Christmas 1996.
12. Jonny Baker interviewed on Radio 4, 7 February 1997.
13. Philippians 2.5–8.
14. See Geoffrey Wainwright, 'The Language of Worship', in C. Jones, G. Wainwright *et al.* (eds), *The Study of Liturgy*. 2nd edn, SPCK, London, 1992, pp. 522–4.
15. Michael Polanyi, *Personal Knowledge*. Routledge and Kegan Paul, London, 1958, 1972, p. 277.
16. Michael Polanyi, *Personal Knowledge*. Routledge and Kegan Paul, London, 1958, 1972, p. 299ff.

Chapter 4

1. Carl Jung, *Modern Man in Search of a Soul*.

Chapter 5

1. Dave Tomlinson, *The Post-Evangelical*. Triangle, London, 1995.

Chapter 6

1. Dave Tomlinson, *The Post-Evangelical*. Triangle, London, 1995.
2. D. W. Bebbington, *Evangelicalism in Modern Britain*. Unwin Hyman, London, 1989.
3. Dave Tomlinson, *The Post-Evangelical*. Triangle, London, 1995, p. 35.